Simple Knitting

a complete how-to-knit workshop with 20 projects

Erika Knight

St. Martin's Griffin
New York

Editorial director Jane O'Shea
Creative director Helen Lewis
Project editor Lisa Pendreigh
Pattern checker Gina Alton
Designer Claire Peters
Photographer Yuki Sugiura
Stylist Charis White
Illustrator Claire Peters
Production director Vincent Smith
Production controller Ruth Deary

Library of Congress Cataloging-in-
Publication Data Available Upon Request

ISBN 978-0-312-66833-4

First U.S. Edition: March 2011

10 9 8 7 6 5 4 3 2 1

Knitting fascinates me. Possibly, this is because it is a simple craft that anyone can master. All you need are two sticks and a continuous thread then, by making a series of interlocking loops, you can create textiles that are both practical and decorative. I find the process of knitting greatly inspiring and never tire of the endless variations and forms its practice may take.

I want to share the simplicity of knitting with you. This book is not an exhaustive encyclopedic how-to-knit tome, instead I have pared down the craft to the essential knitting basics as I see them. For example, I haven't included every possible way to cast on stitches (at the last count, there were twenty-two), instead I believe in mastering just the few ways that are easy, effective, and give the right look I am seeking for a specific design. *Simple Knitting* is knitting my style. In this book I have aimed to provide the basic means to get you knitting—it can be as easy as "in, over, under, off."

In the Materials and Techniques section at the start of this book, I have set out the technical how-to information for the basic knitting methods, but knowing how to work a particular technique is no use in isolation and really only makes sense once it is put into practice. This is where the Project Workshops come in. In fact, providing you can master the simple techniques of casting on, binding off, and working the knit stitch, you can easily make the first few items in the Project Workshops section of this book. There are twenty projects in all, from "getting started" mufflers, thrifty "stitch-practicing" dishcloths and contemporary fold-over pillows, each suitable for the beginner knitter, to more challenging short-row shaping socks, color-blocked blankets, and a vintage-inspired colorwork rose teapot cozy.

Each project provides the opportunity to practice a technique or two by way of a masterclass. It is up to you whether you want to work your way through the projects sequentially, gathering a little momentum with each masterclass, or dip into the projects here and there, honing and perfecting a specific technique.

Soon you will become adept at shaping by increasing, decreasing, and short-row shaping, twisting stitches to form cables, and changing colors while working stripes, stranding, and color blocking.

The variety of projects in *Simple Knitting* very much reflects my personal preference for a pared-down style; simple shapes generally with little decoration in which the texture and shade of each yarn—natural fibers and muted color tones—are integral to my designs. I am, however, exacting about how I finish the final piece: it is essential to take the time to finish a project. But again this is easy; since someone showed me invisible seaming, I seldom use anything else. I share this with you. I've also added a few helpful design tips here and there as notes in the margins, just as I would in my own sketch- and workbooks. I hope they help to gain you an insight into how I approach knitwear design.

As well as honing the skills given in the Materials and Techniques section and practiced in the Project Workshops, I hope you will also enjoy the variety of textures that can be created with knitting. I have included twenty of my very favorite stitches alongside some simple tried-and-tested colorways in the Stitch Library. I hope that they will inspire you to try out different stitch textures and play with colors in order to forge ahead to create your own style.

This book, *Simple Knitting*, is very much my take on the craft. I love the entire process of creating and constructing a knitted fabric. I hope that you will share my love for the craft and, within these pages, find the inspiration to pick up those sticks and, well, just get knitting.

Skill levels

In reality, all the projects in this book are unashamedly simple—that's my style. However, each project has been attributed with a skill level in accordance with the Craft Yarn Council of America's rating system in order to let you know what techniques you are mastering.

BEGINNER

1 Beginner Projects For first-time knitters using basic knit and purl stitches. Minimal shaping.

EASY

2 Easy Projects Using basic stitches, repetitive stitch patterns, simple color changes, and simple shaping and finishing.

INTERMEDIATE

3 Intermediate Projects With a variety of stitches, such as basic cables and lace, simple intarsia, knitting-in-the-round techniques, mid-level shaping and finishing.

EXPERIENCED

4 Experienced Projects Using advanced techniques and stitches, such as short rows, Fair Isle, more intricate intarsia, cables, lace patterns, and numerous color changes.

materials and techniques

Choosing yarns and colors

Due to my many years working within the fashion industry, the selection of materials is paramount to me when designing hand knits; very often it is the yarn or, indeed, the fiber that is the starting point for a project.

I take a lot of time and care to ensure that the fiber, the yarn, the stitch, the weight of the knitted fabric, and the detailing are just right for the proposed design. I believe the time taken over this really pays off, so I always knit up a large swatch of the yarn and ask myself a series of questions. Are the fibers as soft to the touch as I would like? Does the yarn give good stitch clarity? Is the knitted fabric too heavy or too light? Is the yarn and resulting fabric fit for the purpose for which it is intended? Does the overall effect match up to my original design idea? All these questions are especially important, even when designing a seemingly simple piece like the muffler (see pages 64–67) or the fold-over pillow (see pages 70–73).

In fact, the success of a simple design more often than not hinges on the quality of the yarn selected. In the case of the pair of pillows shown together on pages 71 and 72, the contrasting matte mohair and sheeny silk fabrics team up to give these pillows a sumptuous and luxurious feel. The high-quality natural fiber I have used for the pure silk pillow takes the dye-color well and when knitted up creates a fabric that drapes beautifully, while the whisper-fine mohair yarn has an airy, ethereal texture that juxtaposes the smoother silk.

I tend to use natural yarns because of the inherent characteristics of their fibers—they keep the wearer warm in winter yet cool in summer, wicking moisture away from the skin. Moreover natural fibers are light, soft, comfortable to wear, and not without the hint of luxury that comes only from wearing nature's finest—after all, nature does it best!

For the projects in this book, I have chosen a variety of yarns for their unique textures. Primarily, I have selected animal fibers, including the softest baby alpaca, robust extra-fine merino wool, rare British sheeps breed wool, and voluminous light-weight wools, as well as refined silks and diaphanous mohair. Alongside these luxurious animal fibers, sit a small selection of the best natural plant fibers: the versatile staple, organic cotton, and the most ancient of the plant fibers, the exquisite linen.

Whether designing hand-knit garments or homewares, I lean toward an understated color palette of muted tones. Preferring to use the characteristic colors of the natural yarns as a base, I usually introduce stronger "fashion" or seasonal colors only as highlights within the overall scheme. Somehow this just seems like second nature to me now when putting together a color story, hence I return time and time again to my favorite palette of pale milk, oyster and pearl, rose pink, mouse and taupe, misty and smoky blues, inky carbon and the deepest peat brown, with chartreuse and willow supplying little touches of colorful relief.

I love to put opposites together, whether they be color or texture. Natural yarns create an exciting contrast when placed against man-made materials, for example smooth, extra-fine merino wool draped across cool glass or flat, matte cotton cast over highly polished concrete can give vitality and textural interest to the home.

Often a cherished, inherited or found piece of furniture may be the starting point for a project. A favorite worn leather couch deserves a cozy throw, an aging dining chair begs a comfortable pillow—these things can often be my inspiration. Whatever you wish to create and make, whether it is for you to wear or to accessorize your home, within these pages I hope you may find yarns, stitches, designs, techniques, tips, and even color palettes to inspire you, too.

Yarns: fine

Fine yarns offer some of the most refined and delicate materials to knit with—from gossamer-thin mohair to sumptuous cashmere, from hand-dyed silk to paper-feel cotton. Although knitting with fine yarn may be a little more time consuming, the end result is an especially rewarding neat fabric with a clearly defined stitch. Fine-yarn textiles often look less "handmade," more closely resembling a machine-woven fabric with a professional finish.

Opposite (clockwise from top left) A mohair-and-silk-blend yarn (Rowan Kidsilk Haze); a pure silk yarn (Alchemy Silken Straw); a mohair and silk blend yarn (Rowan Kidsilk Haze); a pure silk yarn, which feels like linen (Habu Silk Gima); a pure cashmere yarn (Habu Naturally Dyed Cashmere); a pure cotton yarn, which feels like paper (Habu Cotton Gima)

 Yarn weight: super fine
sock, fingering, baby, UK 4-ply
Average knitted gauge: 27–32 stitches
Recommended needle sizes: 1–3 US
(2.25–3.25mm)

 Yarn weight: fine
sport, baby
Average knitted gauge: 23–26 stitches
Recommended needle sizes: 3–5 US
(3.25–3.75mm)

(These are the most commonly used gauges and needle sizes for these yarn categories.)

Yarns: light and medium

Light and medium are the most popular of all yarn weights as they are easy both to source and to knit with. These categories of yarn include a vast array of fibers— I favor pure fibers and blends—and textures, ranging from smooth matte cottons and linens to naturally marled rare sheeps breed wools. As spinners generally offer a wider palette of colors in lightweight and medium-weight yarns, I tend to use standard double-knitting-weight yarns for my more colorful designs.

 Yarn weight: light
light worsted, DK
Average knitted gauge: 21–24 stitches
Recommended needle sizes: 5–7 US
(3.75–4.5mm)

 Yarn weight: medium
aran, worsted, afghan
Average knitted gauge: 16–20 stitches
Recommended needle sizes: 7–9 US
(4.5–5.5mm)

(These are the most commonly used gauges and needle sizes for these yarn categories.)

Opposite (clockwise from top left) A linen-blend yarn (Rowan Lenpur Linen); a pure alpaca yarn (Rowan Baby Alpaca DK); a pure wool yarn (Rowan British Sheeps Breeds DK Undyed); a pure cotton yarn (Rowan Purelife Organic Cotton DK Naturally Dyed); a mohair-and-silk-blend yarn (Rowan Kidsilk Aura); a linen-blend yarn (Rowan Lenpur Linen); a pure cotton yarn (Rowan Purelife Organic Cotton DK Naturally Dyed)

Yarns: fat

Bulky yarns—or fat yarns as I call them—are some of my favorites. Their sheer volume is inspirational. It's great to learn to knit with bulky-weight yarn on big needles as you're able to see the stitches very clearly and, of course, as the knitting grows very quickly, it is instantly rewarding. I like to use fat yarns for statement projects for the home, such as pillows and throws, where the scale of the yarn adds a certain homespun fun to couches and chairs.

Opposite (clockwise from top left) A wool-blend yarn (Rowan Little Big Wool); a wool-alpaca blend yarn (Blue Sky Alpacas Bulky); a pure cotton yarn made from strips of shirting; a wool-cashmere-blend yarn (Debbie Bliss Como); a merino-blend yarn (Gedifra Merino Grande)

 Yarn weight: bulky
craft, rug, chunky
Average knitted gauge: 12–15 stitches
Recommended needle sizes: 9–11 US (5.5–8mm)

 Yarn weight: super bulky
bulky, roving, UK super chunky
Average knitted gauge: 6–11 stitches
Recommended needle sizes: 11 US and larger (8mm and larger)

(These are the most commonly used gauges and needle sizes for this yarn category.)

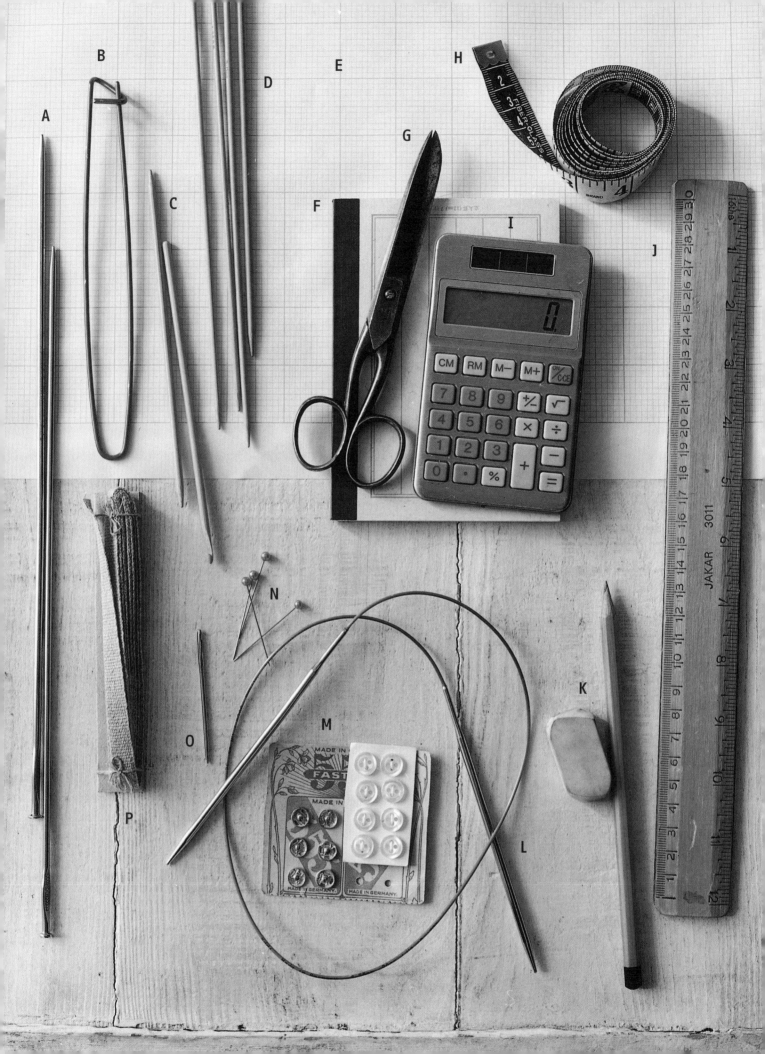

Equipment

A pair of sticks and a continuous length of yarn is all you need to start knitting. Sticks, or rather knitting needles, come in various sizes from fine to fat, in sets of two or four, and attached to wires. There are certain other pieces of equipment that can make the knitting process that little bit easier. Here are some of the most common, and most useful...

A Straight knitting needles: My personal preference in knitting needles is for bamboo, but there is also metal, wood, plastic, and vintage tortoiseshell to choose from; sizes range from fine to fat, most popularly from size 2 US (2.75mm) through to size 19 US (15mm). See page 143 for the full range of sizes.

B Stitch holder: For keeping a set of stitches secure and preventing them from unraveling while they are not being worked. You can also use large safety pins.

C Crochet hook: For picking up dropped stitches or adding crochet edges to projects.

D Set of four double-pointed needles: For working stitches in the round to create a seamless piece of knitting. Gaining popularity are square needles (see page 34).

E Graph paper: For working out small motifs or drawing shapings in pattern instructions.

F Notebook: For recording all those stitch counts and any pattern amendments; we always think that we'll remember them, but then forget them when we come to knit the design again.

G Scissors: For snipping yarns and cutting fabrics and trimmings.

H Tape measure: For checking dimensions. Make sure the tape is not too old or stretched and always measure on a flat surface.

I Calculator: For working out gauges, especially when using a different yarn than the one specified in a pattern, or calculating stitch and row counts when creating your own design.

J Ruler: For accurately measuring a gauge swatch. A ruler is better for this than a tape measure because of its straight, flat edge.

K Pencil and eraser: For recording any notes and amendments in your notebook or directly onto your pattern as you knit, and for amending your amendments.

L Circular knitting needle: Primarily for working in the round, like double-pointed needles. However, many knitters prefer to use a circular needle when knitting throws or other large items as the weight of the knitting can rest on the wire in your lap rather on each needle (see page 35).

M Snaps and buttons: Button styles are a personal preference. Classic mother-of-pearl (in either natural cream or natural gray) is a favorite of mine as I find it complements almost every yarn shade. To avoid making buttonholes, I often use snaps as the fastening and top with a decorative button; this is a particularly good idea for baby garments.

N Glass-headed pins: For pinning together pieces of knitting. The colored heads enable you to find the pins again when sewing seams.

O Blunt-ended yarn needle: For sewing together finished pieces of knitting and weaving in yarn ends. The needle's large eye makes it easier to thread with bulky yarn.

P Woven cotton tape: For strengthening a seam. Use on the inside of a back neck to make a great finishing detail and to prevent stretching (see page 81).

Holding the yarn and needles

Holding the yarn and knitting needles is possibly the most tricky thing to master when learning to knit. The position you adopt will depend on which of the two basic methods you choose. If you opt for the English method, the yarn is held in your right hand. With the Continental method, the yarn is held in your left. It will take a while to work out which method is right for you. I recommend adopting whichever way you find easiest to achieve a flowing, even tension. Everyone knits slightly differently—for example, some knitters find it easier to work the stitches close to the tip of the needles, while others prefer to knit farther back on the shafts. Once you find a comfortable knitting position, your speed will increase and your knitting will become more even.

Continental method

Hold the needle with the stitches in your right hand. Wrap the yarn around your little finger and then around the index finger of your left hand. Move the needle holding the stitches into your left hand. With the working needle in your right hand, control the tension of the yarn with your left index finger.

English method

1 Hold the needle with the stitches in your left hand. With the palm of your right hand facing you, wrap the yarn around your little finger, over the other fingers and then underneath the index finger.

2 With the working needle in your right hand, control the tension of the yarn with your right index finger.
OR
An alternate way of holding the working needle is to place in the crook between thumb and index finger as though holding a pencil.

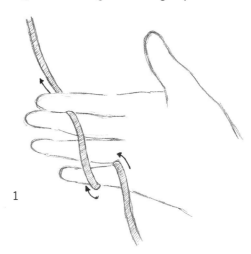

1

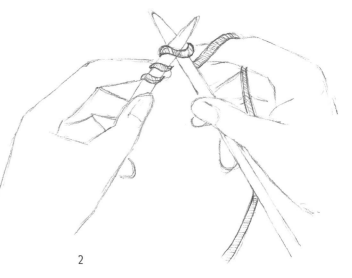

2

Making a slip knot

Before you begin to knit, you must make a foundation row called a cast-on. The first stitch of any cast-on method is a slip knot. There are many methods of casting on. The two examples I give on the following pages are the ones I believe are the most popular, the thumb method and the knit-on method. The thumb method is a double cast-on technique; for this you must leave a predetermined length of yarn free before working the slip knot. A good rule to abide by is to allow a length of approximately three times the planned width of the cast-on edge or 1in/2.5cm per stitch plus a little extra for insurance. For the thumb method, only a 8–10in/20–25cm length of yarn is necessary.

1 Making sure you have left the correct length of yarn, cross over the strands of yarn to make a loop.

2 Pull the strand attached to the ball (known as the working yarn) through the loop to form a second loop.

3 Place the new loop on the knitting needle. Tighten this loop on the needle by pulling on both ends of the yarn. You have formed a slip knit and are now ready to begin one of the cast-on methods on the following pages.

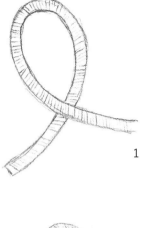

1

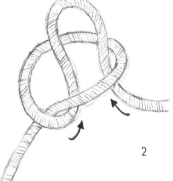

2

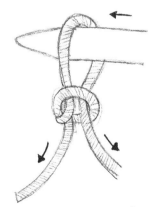

3

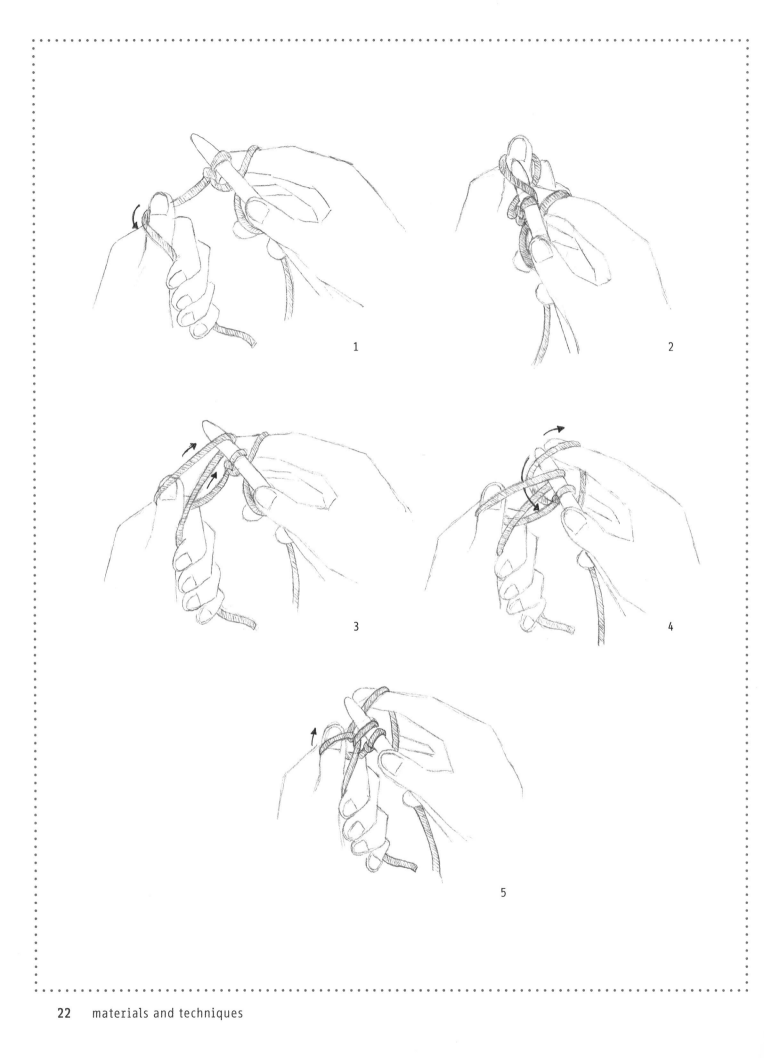

1

2

3

4

5

Casting on

As I have already mentioned, there are over twenty different methods of casting on, but in my opinion you only need the two given here. Each cast-on gives a different visual effect and has different properties; the knit-on cast-on is more elastic and so is good for edges where you need a bit of give, such as the hats on pages 90–93, whereas the double cast on is neat but gives a firmer edge with less elasticity so is better suited to pillows and throws.

Double cast-on—thumb method

Once you have made a slip knot, remembering to leave a long enough length of yarn (see page 21), this simple method of making stitches uses just one knitting needle, a length of yarn and your thumb.

1 Hold the ball end of the yarn along with the knitting needle with the slip knot in your right hand. Take the loose, measured end of the yarn in your left hand and form a loop around your left thumb.

2 Insert the tip of the needle into the loop around your left thumb.

3 With your right hand, wrap the yarn from the ball over the tip of the needle.

4 Pull the needle under and through the loop on your thumb, bringing with it the yarn wrapped around it.

5 Slip the loop off your thumb and gently tighten the stitch by pulling both strands.

Repeat these steps until you have the required number of stitches.

1 Wrap the ball end of the yarn around your left index finger and the measured end around your left thumb. Holding the needle in your right hand, put the tip up through the loop around your thumb.

2 Take it down through the loop around your index finger and then back under the loop on your thumb. Slip your thumb out of its loop, making sure not to drop the loop off the needle. Gently tighten the stitch by pulling both strands.

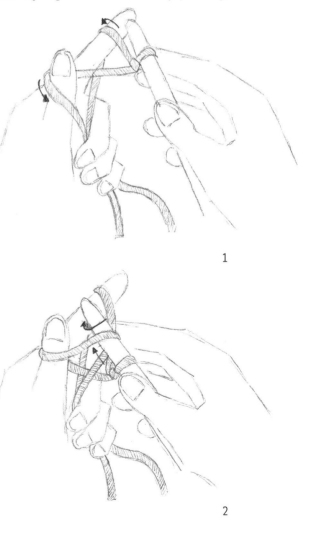

1

2

Knit-on cast-on

The knit-on cast-on method uses two needles and is particularly good for ribbed edges as it provides a sturdy but still elastic edge. Make sure that you do not make the cast-on stitches too tight, especially for ribbing. The knit-on method is one of the most widely used cast-ons.

1 Hold the knitting needle with the slip knot in your left hand and insert the tip of the right-hand needle from left to right and from front to back through the slip knot. Wrap the yarn from the ball up and over the tip of the right-hand needle.

2 With the right-hand needle, draw the yarn through the slip knot.

3 Do not drop the original loop from the left-hand needle.

4 Instead, slip the loop on the right-hand needle onto the left-hand needle to make a new stitch.

5 Next, insert the right-hand needle from left to right and from front to back through the first stitch on the left-hand needle and wrap the yarn around the tip of the right-hand needle.

6 Draw the yarn through. Do not drop the original stitch from the left-hand needle.

7 Transfer the loop on the right-hand needle onto the left-hand needle to make a new stitch, as before.

Repeat the steps 5 and 6 until the required number of stitches have been cast on.

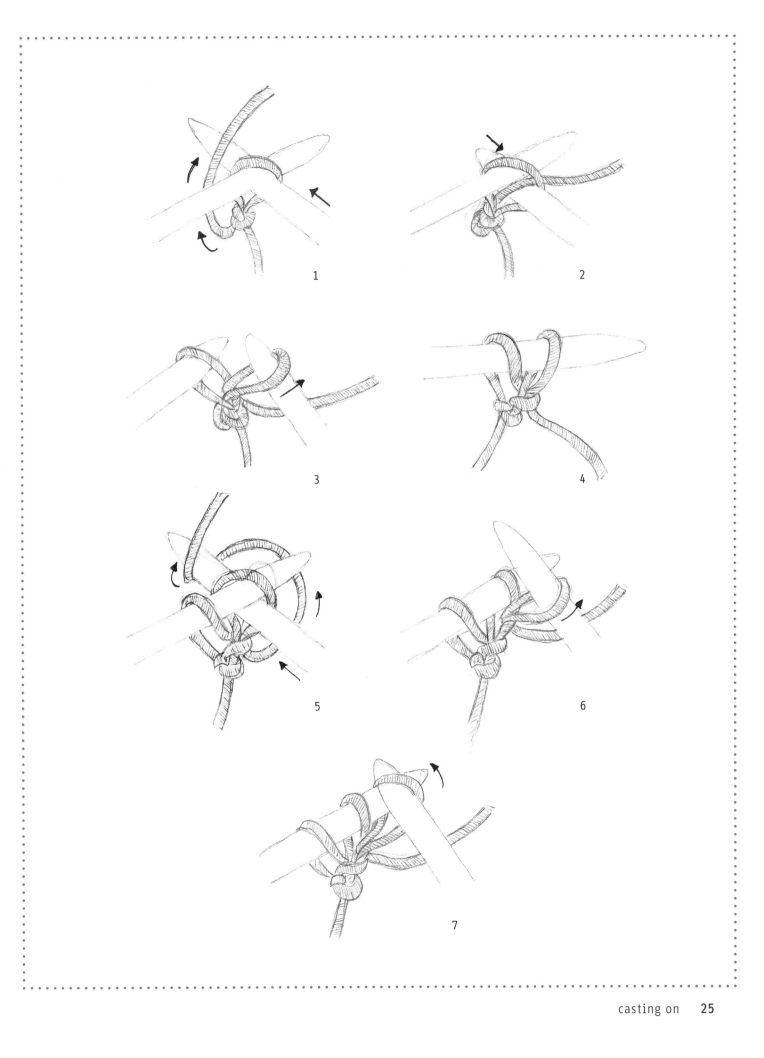

1

2

3

4

5

6

7

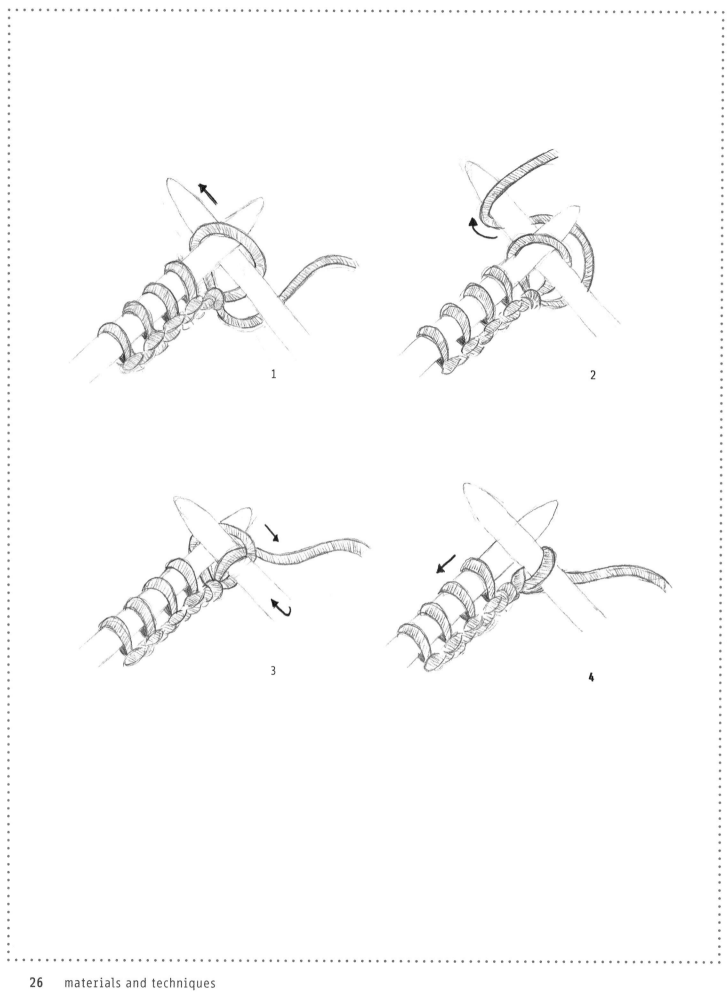

1

2

3

4

Knit one

After casting on the appropriate number of stitches, you can begin to knit your first row. Each stitch is made by the simple four-step process shown here—I always remember it by the chant, "in, over, under, off." Each row is completed by repeating this process until all the stitches on the left-hand needle have been transferred to the right-hand needle. Once you have completed each row, switch the needle holding the worked stitches to your left hand and begin again. Working all the rows in knit stitches will create a fabric known as garter stitch (see page 50), but other combinations of stitches will create different textures (see the Stitch Library on pages 48–61).

1 In Hold the needle with the cast-on stitches in your left hand, then holding the other needle in your right hand, insert the tip of the right-hand needle into the first stitch on the left-hand needle. Pass the needle under the loop facing you and up into the center of the stitch so the needles form an X shape, with the left-hand needle in front of the right-hand needle.

2 Over Holding the working yarn in your right hand, and at the back of the work, wrap the yarn counterclockwise over the tip of the right-hand needle to make a loop.

3 Under Slide the right-hand needle toward you, passing the tip down and out of the center of the stitch on the left-hand needle to pull the loop under and through the first stitch on the left-hand needle.

4 Off Slide the original stitch off the tip of the left-hand needle, leaving the new stitch on the right-hand needle. You have now knitted one stitch to the right-hand needle.

Continental method

Hold the needles using the Continental method (see page 20). Put the tip of the right-hand needle into the first stitch on the left-hand needle. Wrap the working yarn in your left hand over the tip of the right-hand needle. Slide the right-hand needle toward you, passing the tip down and out of the center of the stitch on the left-hand needle to pull the loop under and through the first stitch on the left-hand needle.

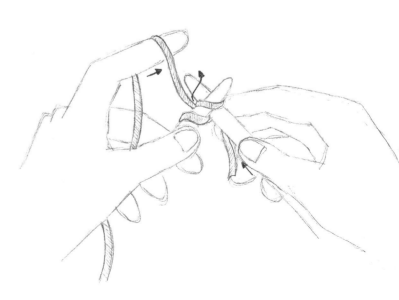

Purl one

This stitch is worked in much the same way as the knit stitch, but with one simple difference: when working the knit stitch, the yarn is held at the back of the work, but with the purl stitch, the yarn is held at the front of the work. Likewise, the purl stitch is made by the simple four-step process shown here. Repeat the process until the row is complete, and all the stitches have been transferred to the right-hand needle. Switch this needle to your left hand before beginning the next row. Combining the knit stitch and the purl stitch provides the basis of all knitted fabrics, including the perennially popular stockinette stitch, which is made by working one row knit, one row purl throughout (see page 50). The simple knit stitch and purl stitch is just about all there is to know!

1 In Hold the needle with the cast-on stitches in your left hand. Holding the other needle in your right hand, and with the working yarn at the front of the work, insert the tip of the right-hand needle into the first stitch on the left-hand needle. Pass the needle from back to front through the center of the first stitch so the needles form an X shape with the right-hand needle in front of the left-hand needle.

2 Over Holding the working yarn in your right hand, and at the front of the work, wrap the yarn counterclockwise over the point of the right-hand needle to make a loop.

3 Under Slide the right-hand needle back and out of the first stitch on the left-hand needle to pull the loop under and through the first stitch on the left-hand needle.

4 Off Slide the original stitch off the point of the left-hand needle, leaving the new stitch on the right-hand needle. You have now purled one stitch to the right-hand needle.

Continental method

Hold the needles using the Continental method (see page 20), with the yarn to the front of the left-hand needle. Put the tip of the right-hand needle into the first stitch from back to front. Wrap the working yarn counterclockwise over the tip of the right-hand needle. Slide the right-hand needle backward, passing the tip down and out of the center of the stitch on the left-hand needle to pull the loop under and through the first stitch on the left-hand needle.

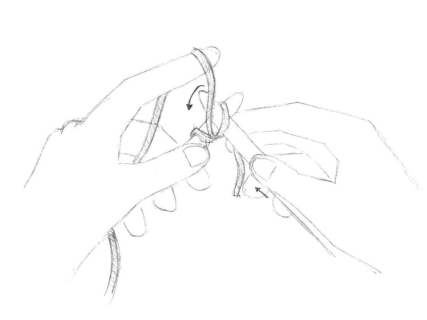

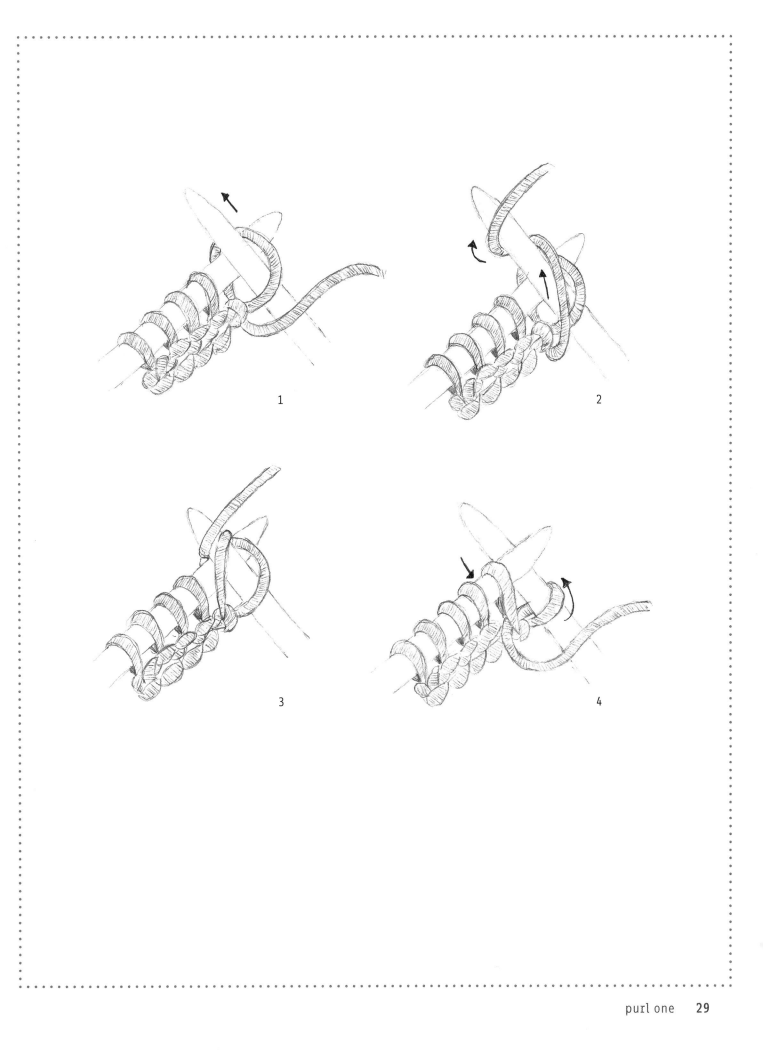

1

2

3

4

Increasing

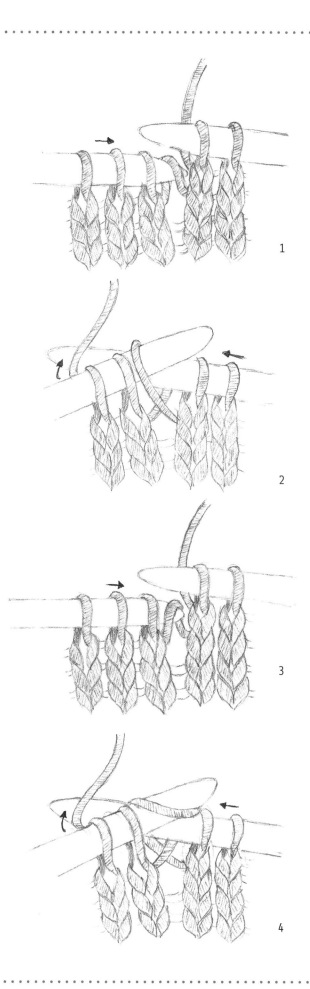

Make one

Adding stitches or taking away stitches—
increasing or decreasing—shapes your knitting.
There are several methods of increasing, but
the simplest way to make an additional stitch
is to pick up the horizontal strand that lies
between two stitches and knit into the back
of it. This type of increase, which is known as
"make one" or "M1" will slope slightly to the
left, however, it is not terribly obvious in the
finished piece. For an alternative method, see
page 96.

Make one (M1) on a knit row—left sloping

1 Work to the position of the increase. With the
tip of the left-hand needle, lift the horizontal
strand that lies between the worked and
unworked stitches, inserting the needle from
front to back under it.

2 Knit into the back of the lifted loop on the
left-hand needle to make one new stitch.

Make one (M1) on a knit row—right sloping

3 Work to the position of the increase. With the
tip of the left-hand needle, lift the horiztonal
strand that lies between the worked and
unworked stitches, inserting the needle from
back to front under it.

4 Knit into the front of the lifted loop on the
left-hand needle to make one new stitch.

Decreasing

Knitting or purling stitches together

The simplest method of taking away stitches, or decreasing, is to knit two stitches together. Knitting the stitches together through the back of the loops forms a left-slanting increase, and knitting through the front of the loops a right-slanting one.

Knit two together (k2tog)—right sloping

1 Instead of inserting the right-hand needle into one stitch on the left-hand needle, insert the tip into the front of the first two stitches at the same time. Wrap the yarn over the tip of the right-hand needle to make a loop. Slide the right-hand needle toward you, passing the tip down and out of the center of the two stitches on the left-hand needle to pull the loop through the stitches on the left-hand needle. Slide the original stitches off the left-hand needle in the usual way, making sure that you drop both stitches from the left-hand needle. There is one stitch on the right-hand needle instead of two.

Knit two together through back loop (k2tog tbl)—left sloping

2 Insert the tip of the right-hand needle into the back of the first two stitches on the left-hand needle. Work in the same way as k2tog, knitting these two stitches together as one.

Purl two together (p2tog)—right sloping

3 Insert the tip of the right-hand needle into the first two stitches on the left-hand needle from back to front. Purl these two stitches together as one.

Purl two together through back loop (p2tog tbl)—left sloping

4 Insert the tip of the right-hand needle into the back of the first two stitches on the left-hand needle. Work in the same way as p2tog, purling these two stitches together as one.

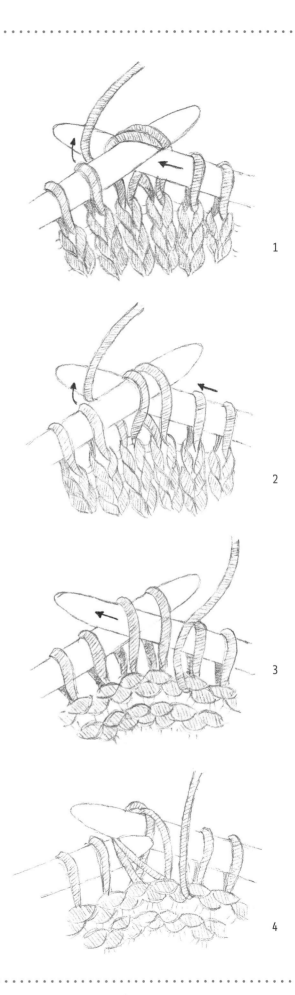

Binding off

Basic knit bind-off

In most instances this is the very last thing you must to do in order to finish your knitting. It is the process that fixes a piece of knitting so that it does not unravel once taken off the needles.

1 At the beginning of your final row, knit the first two stitches as usual. Insert the tip of the left-hand needle into the front loop of the first knitted stitch on the right-hand needle.

2 Lift the first knitted stitch from the right-hand needle over the second knitted stitch on the right-hand needle.

3 Now remove the left-hand needle so only one knitted stitch remains on the right-hand needle. Knit the next stitch on the left-hand needle, so there are two knitted stitches on the right-hand needle again. Repeat these steps, making sure there are never more than two knitted stitches on the right-hand needle.

Work until one knitted stitch remains on the right-hand needle. Cut the working yarn. Pass the end of the yarn through the last loop. Remove the needle and pull on the end of the yarn to tighten.

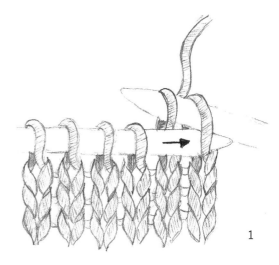

1

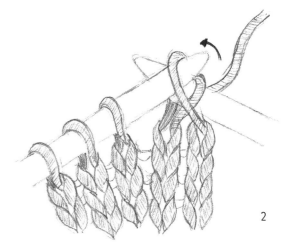

2

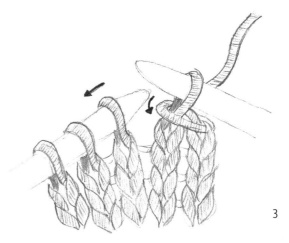

3

Basic purl bind-off

The purl bind-off creates a firm edge and is used on purl stitches.

1 At the beginning of your final row, purl the first two stitches as usual. Insert the tip of the left-hand needle from behind the right-hand needle into the back loop of the first purled stitch on the right-hand needle.

2 Lift the first purled stitch from the right-hand needle over the second purled stitch on the right-hand needle.

3 Now remove the left-hand needle so only one purled stitch remains on the right-hand needle. Purl the next stitch on the left-hand needle so there are two purled stitches on the right-hand needle again. Repeat these steps, making sure there are never more than two purled stitches on the right-hand needle.

Work until one purled stitch remains on the right-hand needle. Cut the working yarn. Pass the end of the yarn through the last loop. Remove the needle and pull on the end of the yarn to tighten.

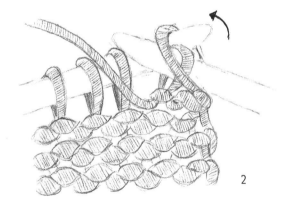

1

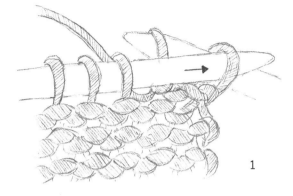

2

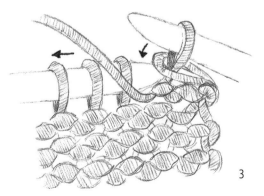

3

Knitting in the round

Knitting in the round can be done on either circular needles or on a set of double-pointed needles. When knitting in the round, the work is joined to make a tubular piece that has no side seams so it is perfect for items such as socks (see pages 110–13). Another advantage is that you only ever work the right side of the fabric, making shaping neater and easier.

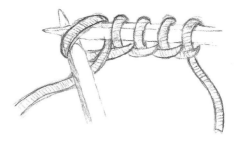

1

Knitting on double-pointed needles

Double-pointed needles have, not surprisingly, points at both ends and come in sets of four or five needles in 6in/18cm and 10in/25cm lengths. It is now possible to get square needles, which are faceted on four sides as opposed to a smooth cylindrical barrel. Some knitters have reported that these square needles help them to achieve more even knitting and reduce any stresses and strains.

1 Cast on the required number of stitches on the first needle, plus one extra. Slip this extra stitch to the next needle as shown. Continue in this way, casting on the required number of stitches on the last needle.

2 Arrange the needles as shown, with the cast-on edge facing the center of the triangle (or square) of stitches.

3 Place a stitch marker or colored thread after the last cast-on stitch to indicate the end of the round. With the free needle, knit the first cast-on stitch, pulling the yarn tight to avoid a gap. Work in a round until you reach the stitch marker. This completes the first round. Slip the marker to the right-hand needle and work the next round.

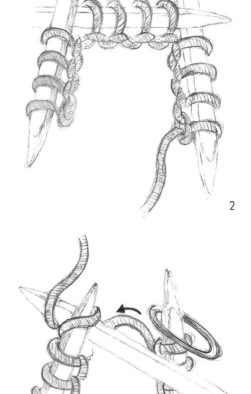

2

3

Knitting on circular needles

Circular needles are available in several lengths. The length used depends on the number of stitches you are working with and the gauge. The needle should be short enough so that the stitches are not stretched when joined.

Circular needles are available with plastic, aluminum or teflon-coated tips, but all have plastic joining wires. If the plastic wire portion of the needle curls, immerse it in hot water to straighten it before you begin to knit. When you join your work, make sure that the stitches are not twisted around the needle. A twisted cast-on cannot be rectified once you have worked a round. To help you keep the stitches untwisted, keep the cast-on edge facing the center, or work one row before joining the stitches, then sew the gap closed later.

To identify the beginning of each new round, place a marker or differently colored thread between the first and last cast-on stitches before joining. Slip the marker before each subsequent round.

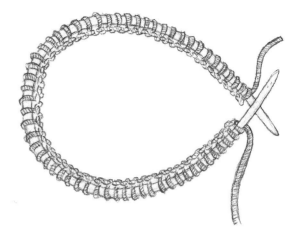

Cast on as you would for straight knitting. Distribute the stitches evenly around the needle, making sure not to twist them. Place a stitch marker or colored thread after the last cast-on stitch to indicate the end of the round. Hold the needle tip with the last cast-on stitch in your right hand and the tip with the first cast-on stitch in your left hand. Knit the first cast-on stitch, pulling the yarn tight to avoid a gap. Work in a round until you reach the stitch marker. This completes the first round. Slip the marker to the right-hand needle and work the next round.

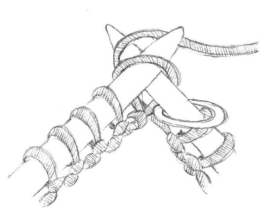

Making a gauge swatch

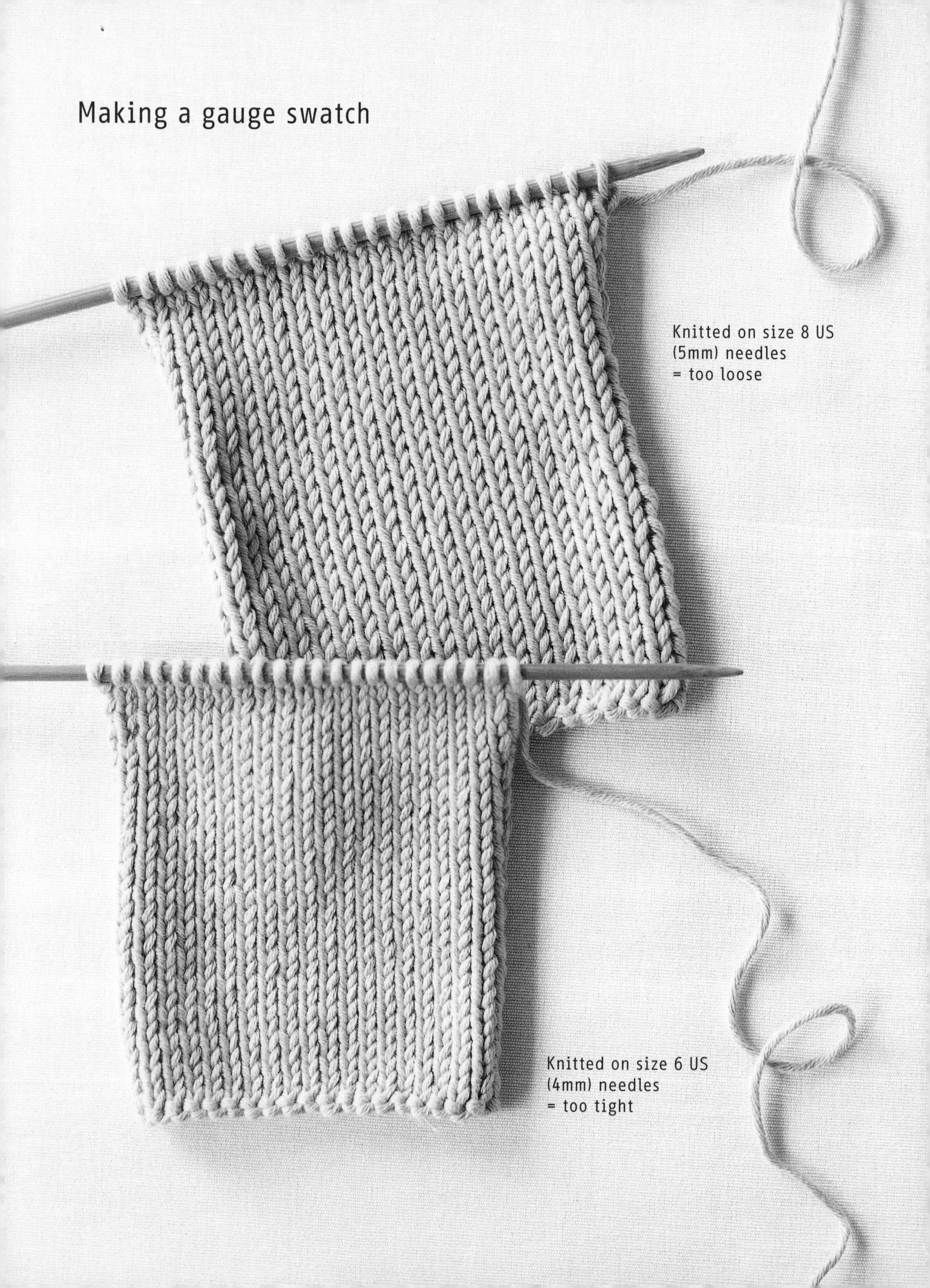

Knitted on size 8 US
(5mm) needles
= too loose

Knitted on size 6 US
(4mm) needles
= too tight

Knitted on size 7 US
(4.5mm) needles =
just right

It is crucial to check your gauge before you embark on any project. The stitch gauge is the number of stitches and rows to 1in/2.5cm or 4in/10cm. The gauge determines the measurements of a garment, so it is critical you obtain the same number of rows and stitches as the pattern states.

A small difference over 4in/10cm can add up to a considerable amount over the complete width of the knitted garment. If your gauge is looser or tighter than the one stated in the knitting pattern, your garment will be larger or smaller than the specified size. So taking the time to work a gauge square before you start can save a lot of heartache later on.

The size of the stitch depends on the yarn, the size of the knitting needles, and your control of the yarn. It can also depend on mood—many knitters hold the yarn with a tighter tension when stress levels are high!

Using the same yarn and needles and stitch that the gauge has been measured over in the pattern, knit a sample at least 5in/13cm square.

Measuring a gauge swatch

Smooth out the square on a flat surface. To check stitch gauge, place a ruler (a cloth tape measure can be less accurate) horizontally on the fabric and mark 4in/10cm with pins. Count the number of stitches between the pins. To check row gauge, place a ruler vertically, mark 4in/10cm with pins and count the number of rows. If the number of stitches and rows is greater than it says in the pattern, your gauge is tighter. This can usually be regulated by using larger needles. If the number of stitches is fewer than the specified number, your gauge is looser and you should change to smaller needles. A word of caution: your gauge may change from that of your sample when knitting the actual garment, as your knitting can alter when working across more stitches.

Abbreviations

Following is a list of the most commonly used abbreviations within knitting patterns. In addition, special abbreviations may also be included at the start of a pattern, such as the directions for a specific cable stitch, which are not necessarily on this list. Generally, definitions of any special abbreviations used are given at the beginning of a book or pattern.

[ ]	work instructions within brackets as many times as directed
( )	work instructions within parentheses for your chosen size
*	repeat instructions up to or following the single asterisk as directed
* *	repeat instructions following the double asterisks as directed
alt	alternate
approx	approximately
beg	begin/beginning
bet	between
C4B	cable four back—slip next 2 stitches onto cable needle and hold at back of work, knit 2 stitches, then knit 2 stitches from cable needle
C4F	cable four front—slip next 2 stitches onto cable needle and hold at front of work, knit 2 stitches, then knit 2 stitches from cable needle
C8B	cable eight back—slip next 4 stitches onto cable needle and hold at back of work, knit 4 stitches, then knit 4 stitches from cable needle
C8F	cable eight front—slip next 4 stitches onto cable needle and hold at front of work, knit 4 stitches, then knit 4 stitches from cable needle
C12B	cable twelve back—slip next 6 stitches onto cable needle and hold at back of work, knit 6 stitches, then knit 6 stitches from cable needle
C12F	cable twelve front—slip next 6 stitches onto cable needle and hold at front of work, knit 6 stitches, then knit 6 stitches from cable needle
CC	contrasting color
cm	centimeter(s)
cn	cable needle
CO	cast on
cont	continue/continuing
dec	decrease/decreases/decreasing
DK	double knitting (a standard UK yarn weight)
dpn	double-pointed needle(s)
foll	follow/follows/following
g	gram(s)
in	inch(es)
inc	increase/increases/increasing
k or K	knit

k1b	knit into stitch below next stitch
k2tog	knit 2 stitches together
k2tog tbl	knit 2 stitches together through back loops
kb1	knit into back of next stitch
kfb	knit into front and back of next stitch
kwise	knitwise
LH	left hand
lp(s)	loop(s)
m	meter(s)
M1	make one—a knitwise increase (see pages 30 and 39)
M1 p-st	make one—a purlwise increase
MC	main color
mm	millimeter(s)
oz	ounce(s)
p or P	purl
patt	pattern; work in pattern
p2tog	purl 2 stitches together
p2tog tbl	purl 2 stitches together through back loops
psso	pass slipped stitch over
pwise	purlwise
rem	remain/remains/remaining
rep	repeat(s)/repeating
rev St st	reverse stockinette stitch
RH	right hand
rnd(s)	round(s)
RS	right side
skp	slip 1, knit 1, pass slipped stitch over (also known as psso)—a one-stitch decrease
sk2p	slip 1, knit 2 together, pass slipped stitch over the knit 2 together—a two-stitch decrease
sl	slip
sl1k	slip 1 knitwise
sl1p	slip 1 purlwise
sl st	slip stitch(es)
ssk	slip, slip, knit these 2 stiches together— a one-stitch decrease
sssk	slip, slip, slip, knit 3 stitches together
st(s)	stitch(es)
st st	stockinette stitch
tbl	through back loop
tog	together
WS	wrong side
yb	yarn to back of work between two needles
yd(s)	yard(s)
yf	yarn to front of work between two needles
yo	yarn over; yarn over right needle to make a new stitch

Terminology

Sometimes understanding a knitting pattern can seem like battling with a foreign language. While it may seem baffling at first, once you pick up a few key phrases you will be fluent!

Alt rows this is used when you have to work something on every alternate row, most usually shaping

At front edge the edge that meets in the center, sometimes the edge with a buttonhole or button band

At side edge the edge you will sew to another piece of knitting, usually referred to when knitting a cardigan

At the same time used when you are shaping a garment and you need to do different shapings on different edges. For example, you may be decreasing for the armhole and at the same time decreasing for the neck

Bind off to finish off an edge and keep stitches from unraveling by lifting the first stitch over the second, the second over the third, and so on

Bind off in rib maintain the rib patterns as you bind off (knit the knit stitches; purl the purl stitches)

Cast on form a foundation row by making a specified number of loops on the knitting needle

Cont in patt/as set continue to work in the pattern that has been established in the preceding rows

Decrease reduce the number of stitches in a row (for example, knit 2 together; purl 2 together)

Increase add to the number of stitches in a row (for example, knit in front and back of stitch)

Integral edge a number of stitches worked in a contrasting stitch or texture at the same time as the main knitting to give a "seamless" finish (for example, buttonbands or edges of a throw)

Knit one stitch below (k1b) insert the right-hand needle into the next stitch but in the row below the stitch on the left-hand needle. Then knit the stitch as normal (see right)

Knitwise insert the needle into the stitch as if you were going to knit it

Make one with tip of needle, lift strand between last stitch worked and next stitch on left-hand needle, place strand on left-hand needle and knit into back of it to increase one stitch

On 4th and on every foll 6th row usually used for shaping: work three rows then work the decrease or increase (whichever is specified) on the fourth row. Work five more rows then decrease or increase as specified in the sixth row. You then continue to work five rows and increase or decrease on the sixth row until you have completed the required number of increases or decreases

Pick up and knit/purl knit or purl into the loops along an edge for the numbers of stitches stated

Place markers loop a piece of contrasting yarn or stitch marker onto the needle or ends of row

Purlwise insert the needle into the stitch as if you were going to purl it

Rep from * repeat the instructions given after the *

Reverse shaping this usually appears in the pattern for a garment where one half, such as the right front, must mirror the other half, the left front

Selvage edge/stitch the edge stitch which helps to make seaming easier

Slip stitch pass a stitch from the left-hand to the right-hand needle as if to purl without working it

Turn stop working at this point (ignore the stitches unworked on the left-hand needle), turn and work on these stitches as instructed

Work without shaping/work even continue in specified pattern without increasing or decreasing

Work to last 2 sts work across the row until there are two stitches (or number stated) on the left-hand needle

Yarn over make a new stitch by placing the yarn over the right-hand needle (yo)

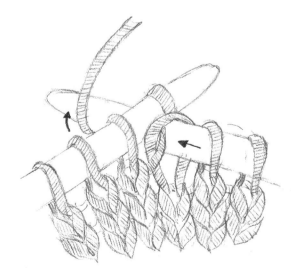

Seams

A beautiful piece of knitting can be ruined
by poor finishing, so take ample time when
sewing seams. Alongside backstitch (see page
73), I almost exclusively use mattress stitch—an
invisible seaming method—for joining seams.
Unlike other hand-knit designers, I prefer not
to use the yarn end from the piece for seams.
Instead, I use a fresh length of yarn or thread.
This is for the simple reason that it is easier to
close the seam by gently pulling the thread from
both ends. When pulled from just the one end,
the strain can often lead to the yarn breaking.

Joining two selvages

Thread a blunt-ended yarn needle with a length
of yarn. With right sides up, lay the two pieces
of knitting to be joined selvage to selvage. On
one piece, from the front, take the needle under
the first two bars that divide the stitches from
the ones in the rows above. Take the needle
across to the other piece and then, from the
front, take the needle under the equivalent
two bars. Continue in this way, switching from
one piece to the other, picking up two bars
each time, until the seam is completed. Stop at
regular intervals of approximately 2in/5cm to
gently pull the thread to close the seam.

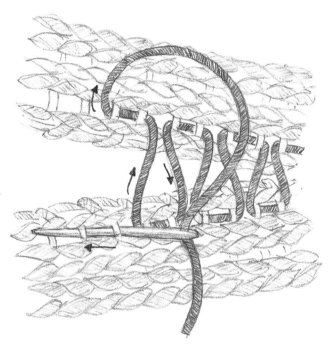

Joining a bound-off edge to a selvage

Thread a blunt-ended yarn needle with a length
of yarn. With right sides up, lay the two pieces
of knitting to be joined bound-off edge to
selvage. On the bound-off edge, from the back
to the front, take the needle through the center
of the first stitch. Next, take the needle under
one or two bars (depending on whether or not
the stitch is as wide as it is long) between the
first and second stitches of the selvage and
then back through the center of the same stitch
on the bound-off edge. Continue in this way,
switching from bound-off edge to selvage, until
the seam is completed.

Joining a rib seam with knit stitch edges

With right sides up, lay the two pieces of knitting to be joined selvage to selvage. On the one piece, from the front, take the needle under the bar in the center of the first knit stitch. Take the needle across to the other piece and then, from the front, take the needle under the equivalent bar. Continue in this way, gently pulling the thread, to form one complete knit stitch along the seam.

Joining a rib seam with purl stitch edges

Skip the purl stitch at the edge of each piece and join the seam at the center of the first knit stitches, as for joining two knit stitch edges.

Joining a rib seam with knit and purl stitch edges

Skip the purl stitch at the edge of one piece of knitting and join the seam at the center of the first knit stitches, as for joining two knit stitch edges.

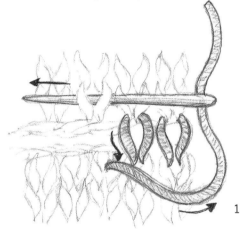

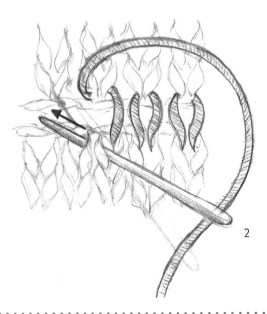

Joining two bound-off edges

1 Thread a blunt-ended yarn needle with a length of yarn. With right sides up, lay the two pieces of knitting to be joined with the bound-off edges butted together. On the lower piece, from the back to the front, take the needle through the center of the first stitch just below the bound-off edge. Next, take the needle through the center of the first stitch on the upper piece and out through the center of the next stitch.

2 Next, take the needle through the center of the first stitch on the lower piece again and out through the center of the next stitch to the left. Continue in this way, switching from the lower piece to the upper piece, until the seam is completed.

Troubleshooting

So what do you do when things go wrong? Even the best of knitters occasionally drop a stitch or go astray from a pattern and have to unravel their work. If it happens to you, don't despair and don't panic. With a dropped stitch, keep the work as still as possible so as not to unravel the stitch farther or ensure that it doesn't travel by securing it with a safety pin. And on unraveling mistakes, although it may be demoralizing at the time to undo lots of rows, it is better to correct an error right away than continue regardless and regret it forever more!

Picking up a dropped stitch on a knit row

Work to the dropped stitch. Make sure the dropped stitch is sitting in front of the loose horizontal strand of the row above. Put the tip of a crochet hook into the loop of the dropped stitch from front to back and then, using the hook, catch the horizontal strand and pull it through the stitch. The strand has now become a stitch. Repeat as many times as necessary until the dropped stitch has been picked up through all the rows. Put the last stitch picked up onto the left-hand needle to be knitted.

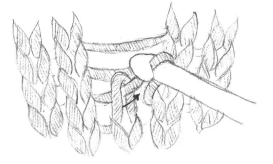

Picking up a dropped stitch on a purl row

Work to the dropped stitch. Make sure the dropped purl stitch is sitting behind the loose horizontal strand of the row above. Put the tip of a crochet hook into the loop of the dropped stitch from back to front and then, using the hook, catch the horizontal strand and pull it through the stitch. The strand has now become a stitch. Repeat as many times as necessary until the dropped stitch has been picked up through all the rows. Put the last stitch picked up onto the left-hand needle to be purled.

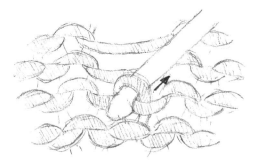

Unraveling stitch by stitch on a knit row

Put the tip of the left-hand needle into the front of the first stitch below the first stitch on the right-hand needle. Let the stitch drop off the right-hand needle and tug the yarn to pull the stitch free. Repeat this until you reach the mistake to be corrected.

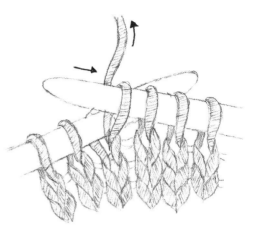

Unraveling stitch by stitch on a purl row

Put the tip of the left-hand needle into the front of the first stitch below the first stitch on the right-hand needle. Let the stitch drop off the right-hand needle and tug the yarn to pull the stitch free. Repeat this until you reach the mistake to be corrected.

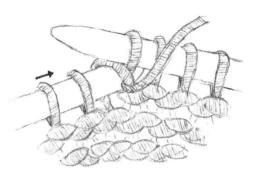

Unraveling several rows

Take the knitting off both needles and slowly and carefully pull out the yarn, unraveling the stitches, until you reach the row with the mistake. Holding the knitting in your left hand and the needle in your right, put the tip of the needle into the first stitch of the unraveled loops. Continue in this way until all the stitches are back on the needle.

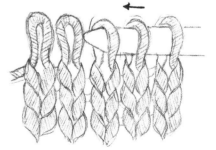

Understanding patterns

When it comes to understanding knitting patterns, there are many shared conventions and terminology. Though designers and yarn companies may use slight variations in their styles, the same information is always given. Before purchasing yarn for any project, read through the pattern to ensure you understand exactly what is needed.

Size

For homewares and accessories, patterns usually come in a single size. For garments, however, I like to give a choice of sizes ranging from extra small to extra large. For the V-neck and cardigan on pages 134–41, I have given the actual measurements of the finished knitted piece as well as the recommended bust measurement each size is designed to fit. Depending on the intended fit of a garment—whether it is loose or tight fitting—these two measurements will not necessarily be the same.

Materials

The pattern specifies what type of yarn is needed for the project, along with the total number of balls. When the pattern is for a garment that comes in different sizes, the number of balls needed for each size will be stated. Also given in the materials list will be the size of knitting needles required, which could be one or more pairs, as well as any extras, such as buttons and zippers.

Gauge

The stitch gauge, indicates how many stitches and rows you must have to a certain measurement, usually 4in/10cm square. Your gauge needs to be correct to achieve the exact dimensions given in a pattern (see pages 36–37 for more on this). Achieving an exact gauge is less critical for a throw or a pillow than for a garment. A difference in gauge when knitting a garment will not only affect the finishied dimensions but will also alter on the amount of yarn needed to complete the project.

Pattern instructions

The pattern works through the individual elements of the project, giving all the necessary instructions for each part. Every pattern begins with the size of needles and shade of yarn used (if more than one color is used), and number of stitches cast on. The pattern will continue to outline, row by row, the stitch pattern to follow and indicate when any shaping or other details, such as buttonholes, should be worked. It can take a while to become familiar with the language of knitting patterns, so on pages 38 and 39 I have listed the most commonly used abbreviations and added a glossary of phrases.

When following any pattern, you need to be aware of the different usage of parentheses ( ) and brackets [ ]. Parentheses ( ) contain the different measurements or stitches given for multiple sizes. The sizes given for the V-neck on pages 134–37 are extra-small, small, medium, large, and extra-large. If you choose to knit the medium size, then you need to follow the third size given in the pattern instructions. So where the instructions state: *Using 3 US (3.25mm) needles, cast on 97 (103: 109: 115: 119) sts*—to knit the medium size, you must cast on 109 stitches, the third number listed. The first size is always shown outside the parentheses and the remaining sizes within them. Likewise, parentheses are used for specific measurements within a pattern of different sizes. So where the instructions state: *Cont in St st until work measures 14 1/2 (15: 15 1/4: 15 3/4: 16)in/37 (38: 39: 40: 41)cm*—to knit the medium size, again, you must follow the third measurement listed which is 15 1/4in/39cm.

Be aware that many knitting patterns also contain brackets [ ]. These have nothing to do with sizing but relate to repeating instructions (see page 38).

Finishing

This tells you how to sew together your completed pieces in order to get the best finish.

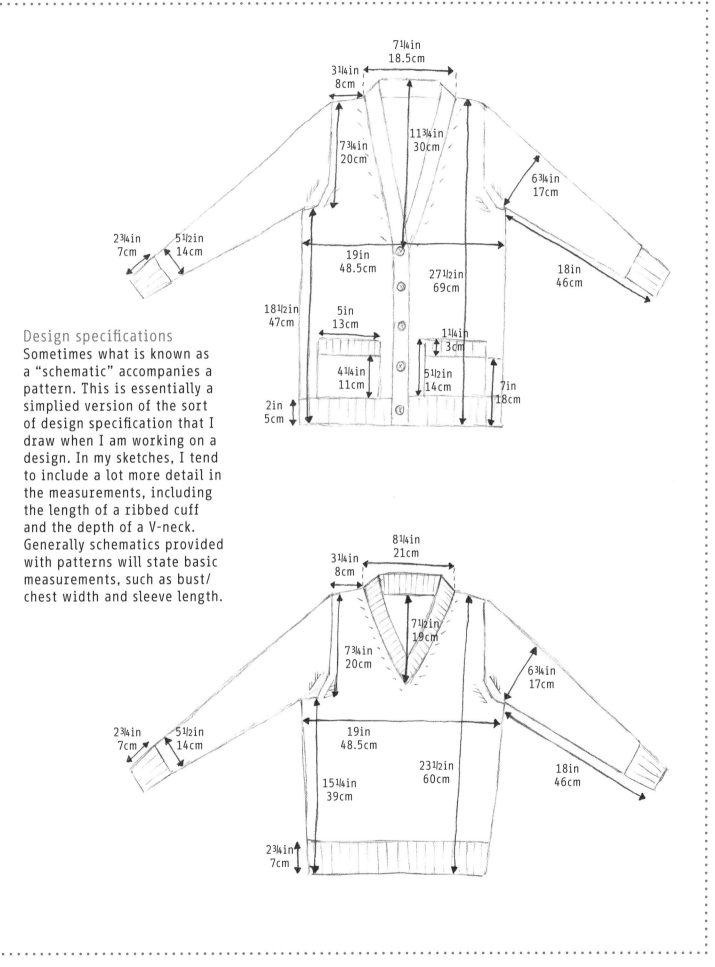

Design specifications

Sometimes what is known as a "schematic" accompanies a pattern. This is essentially a simplied version of the sort of design specification that I draw when I am working on a design. In my sketches, I tend to include a lot more detail in the measurements, including the length of a ribbed cuff and the depth of a V-neck. Generally schematics provided with patterns will state basic measurements, such as bust/chest width and sleeve length.

Reading charts

Instead of being written out row by row using the abbreviations and terms on pages 44–45, a stitch pattern can be represented as a chart on graph paper. Each square of the chart represents one stitch, and each line of squares represents one row of knitting. Different stitches are denoted by either a color or a symbol, explained in a key.

With both types of chart, the right-side rows (or odd-numbered knit rows) are read from right to left, while the wrong-side rows (or even-numbered purl rows) are read from left to right. The rows of the chart are read from the bottom to the top.

Likewise, colorwork instructions can either be written out in full within the pattern or represented as a chart. The various shades of yarn that make up the colorwork motif are represented either as a shaded color (right) or as a symbol (far right).

Key

C Brown

A Light Gray

B Dark Gray

C Brown

A Light Gray

B Dark Gray

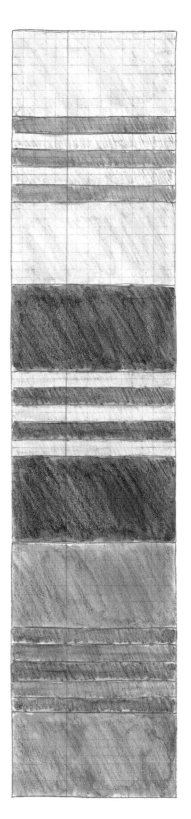

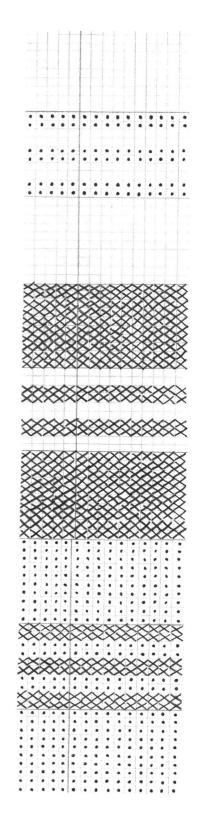

Aftercare

After investing so much time creating a hand knit, great care should be taken in the laundering. How frequent a garment needs washing depends on how it is worn or used. Many of the projects in this book may not need laundering on a regular basis. If it does, the yarn you use must be able to withstand this, but this does not necessarily mean that all yarns must be machine washable. Look at the labels: those on most commercial yarns have instructions for washing or dry cleaning, drying, and pressing. So, for a project knitted in a single yarn, a quick look at the label will tell you how to care for it. If you wish to work with several yarns in one project, the aftercare requires a little more thought. If one label states dry clean only, then dry clean the garment.

Washing

If in doubt about whether or not your knitting is washable, then make a little swatch of the yarns. Wash this to see if the fabric is affected by being immersed in water or not, watching for shrinkage and stretching. If satisfied with the results, go ahead and wash the knitting by hand in lukewarm water. Never use hot water, as this will felt your fabric, and you will not be able to return it to its pre-washed state. In particular, wool tends to react to major changes in temperature.

When washing any knitted item, handle it carefully. There should be enough water to cover the garment completely and the soap should be thoroughly dissolved before immersing it. If you need to sterilize a badly soiled or stained garment, then use a proprietary brand of sterilizer for this purpose.

As a precaution, test wash any trims you use before you make up the garment with them. Nothing is more infuriating than to spoil an entire garment because the trim colors run in the wash. Natural fibers such as wool, cotton and silk are usually better washed by hand, and in pure soap, than in a machine. Should you decide to wash any knitted garment in a machine, place it inside a pillowcase as an extra precaution. Soap flakes are kinder to sensitive skins than most detergents, provided all traces of the soap are removed in the rinsing process.

Rinsing

Squeeze out any excess water, never wring it out. Rinse thoroughly, until every trace of soap is removed; any left will mat the fibers and may irritate the skin. Use at least two changes of water or continue until the water is clear and without soap bubbles. Keep the rinsing water the same temperature as the washing water.

Spinning

Garments can be rinsed on a short rinse and spin as part of the normal washing machine program for delicate fabrics. Again, as an extra precaution, place the item to be spun inside a pillowcase.

Drying

Squeeze the garment between towels or fold in a towel and gently spin. Do not hang wet knitting up to dry, as the weight of the water will stretch it out of shape. To dry, lay the knitting out flat on top of a towel, which will absorb some of the moisture. Ease the garment into shape. Dry away from direct heat and leave flat until completely dry.

Pressing

When the garment is dry, ease it into shape. Check the yarn label before pressing your knitting as most fibers only require a little steam, and the iron should be applied gently. Alternatively, press with a damp cloth between the garment and the iron.

Removing stains

Stains are a fact of life. The best solution with any stain is to remove the garment while the stain is still wet and soak it thoroughly in cold, never hot, water. Failing that, use a proprietary stain remover.

stitch library

basic stitches

Worked over any number of stitches

Knit every row.

Garter Stitch

- the first stitch to master
- creates a firm, neat fabric
- rows look like little "waves"
- when counting rows, one row of "waves" is two rows of knitting

Worked over any number of stitches

Row 1 (RS) Knit.
Row 2 Purl.
Rep these 2 rows.

Stockinette Stitch

- creates a basic smooth fabric, with one side of tiny V's, most often called the right side
- the V's are easy to count when checking gauge

Reverse Stockinette Stitch

- creates a good alternative texture
- looks similar to garter stitch but makes a lighter fabric

Worked over any number of stitches

Row 1 (RS) Purl.
Row 2 Knit.
Rep these 2 rows.

Twisted Stockinette Stitch

- this stitch creates a simple surface texture
- when I started to knit, I was working twisted stockinette stitch by mistake

Worked over any number of stitches

Row 1 (RS) Knit into back of every stitch.
Row 2 Purl.
Rep these 2 rows.

rib stitches

K1, P1 Rib
- a classic stitch to knit
- usually the beginning stitch for sweaters and cardigans
- gives elasticity to cuffs, lower borders, and collars

K2, P2 Rib
- a variation on basic rib; probably the most popular
- great for close-fitting garments and "New Yorker" style hats

Worked over an even number of stitches

Row 1 * K1, p1, rep from * to end.
Rep this row.

Worked over an odd number of stitches

Row 1 K1, * P1, K1, rep from * to end.
Row 2 P1, * K1, P1, rep from * to end.
Rep these 2 rows.

Worked over a multiple of 4 sts

Row 1 * K2, p2, rep from * to end.
Rep this row.

Worked over a multiple of 4 sts plus 2 sts

Row 1 K2, * p2, k2, rep from * to end.
Row 2 P2, * k2, p2, rep from * to end.
Rep these 2 rows.

K3, P2 Rib

- one of my favorite rib set-ups
- I prefer to use odd-number ribs, especially for menswear

Worked over a multiple of 5 sts plus 3 sts

Row 1 * K3, p2, rep from * to last 3 sts, k3.
Row 2 P3, * K2, p3, rep from * to end.
Rep these 2 rows.

Worked over a multiple of 5 sts plus 2 sts

Row 1 * P2, k3, rep from * to last 2 sts, p2.
Row 2 * K2, p3, rep from * to last 2 sts, k2.
Rep these 2 rows.

Slip Stitch Rib

- creates an interesting linen-like surface
- requires concentration in taking the yarn to the front and back

Worked over a multiple of 2 sts plus 1 st

Row 1 (WS) Purl.
Row 2 K1, * yf, sl 1 purlwise, yb, k1, rep from * to end.
Rep these 2 rows.

texture stitches

Worked over any number of stitches

Rows 1 (RS), 3 (RS), and 4 (WS) Knit.
Row 2 Purl.
Rep these 4 rows.

Purl Bar Stitch

- an easy and effective way to lift a plain garment or project with simple texture rows
- creates what is called a "semi-plain" textile

Worked over a multiple of 4 sts plus 3 sts

Row 1 (RS) K1, * p1, k3, rep from * to last 2 sts, p1, k1.
Row 2 Purl.
Row 3 K3, p1, rep from * to last 3 sts, k3.
Row 4 Purl.
Rep these 4 rows.

Dot Stitch

- derives its inspiration from woven fabric
- creates a discreet knobbly-look pattern

Mock Rib Stitch

- a useful replacement for rib that doesn't pull in the fabric
- the reverse creates an interesting basketweave effect

Worked over a multiple of 2 sts plus 1 st

Row 1 (RS) K1, * p1, k1, rep from * to end.
Row 2 P1, * keeping yarn at front of work sl 1 purlwise, p1, rep from * to end.
Rep these 2 rows.

Uneven Rib Stitch

- a staggered rib stitch that has pronounced lines of single knit stitches
- this stitch gives the illusion of greater depth than other ribs

Worked over a multiple of 4 sts plus 3 sts

Row 1 K2, p2, rep from * to last 3 sts, k2, p1.
Rep this row.

texture
stitches

Worked over a multiple of 2 sts plus 1 st

Row 1 K1, * p1, k1, rep from * to end.
Rep this row.

Seed Stitch

– *reversible stitch*
– *firm texture*
– *suitable for both fine and fat yarns*

Worked over a multiple of 2 sts plus 1 st

Row 1 (WS) P1, * kb1, p1, rep from * to end.
Row 2 Knit.
Row 3 * Kb1, p1, rep from * to last st, kb1.
Row 4 Knit.
Rep these 4 rows.

kb1 = knit into back of next stitch

Double Rice Stitch

– *beautiful stitch to work in fine cotton*

Herringbone Stitch

- makes a natural decorative edge
- perfect stitch for scarves and sweaters

Worked over a multiple of 7 sts plus 1 st

Row 1 (WS) Purl.
Row 2 * K2tog, k2, k1b tbl then knit st above, k2, rep from * to last st, k1.
Row 3 Purl.
Row 4 K3, k1 tbl then knit st above, k2, k2tog, * k2, k1b tbl then knit st above, k2, k2tog, rep from * to end.
Rep these 4 rows.

k1b tbl = knit into back of stitch below next stitch

Tweed Stitch

- reversible stitch
- firm fabric for homewares projects
- go up a size needle for a more fluid fabric

Worked over a multiple of 2 sts plus 1 st

Row 1 (RS) K1, * yf, sl1 purlwise, yb, k1, rep from * to end.
Row 2 P2, * yb, sl1 purlwise, yf, p1, rep from * to last st, p1.
Rep these 2 rows.

cable stitches

See abbreviations on page 38 for cable stitches

Worked over a panel of 4 sts on reverse stockinette stitch

Row 1 (RS) Knit.
Row 2 Purl.
Row 3 C4B.
Row 4 Purl.
Rep these 4 rows.
The cable twists to the right.
To work the cable to the left, in row 3 instead of C4B, work C4F where the cable needle is held at the front of work.

4-Stitch Cable

- the simplest of all the cables
- use in little neat rows
- reminiscent of the traditional cricket sweaters

Worked over a panel of 8 sts on reverse stockinette stitch

Row 1 (RS) Knit.
Row 2 Purl.
Rows 3 and 4 Rep rows 1 and 2.
Row 5 C8B.
Row 6 Purl.
Rows 7–10 [Rep rows 1 and 2] twice.
Rep these 10 rows.
The cable twists to the right.
To work the cable to the left, in row 5 instead of C8B, work C8F where the cable needle is held at the front of the work.

8-Stitch Cable

- although simple to do, this cabling looks very clever!
- it is easy to twist cables to either the right or the left

Worked over a panel of
12 sts on reverse
stockinette stitch

Row 1 (RS) Knit.
Row 2 Purl.
Row 3 C12B.
Row 4 Purl.
Rows 5–16 [Rep rows 1
and 2] 6 times.
Rep these 16 rows.

Large Cable

- oversized cables add an extra dynamic
- a sculptural stitch perfect for homewares, garments, and accessories

Cable Braid

- twisting stitches to both the front and the back sounds more complex than it really is
- braided cables can travel all over knitting

Worked over a panel of
12 sts on reverse
stockinette stitch

Row 1 (RS) Knit.
Row 2 Purl.
Row 3 C8F, k4.
Row 4 Purl.
Rows 5–8 [Rep rows 1
and 2] twice.
Row 9 K4, C8B.
Row 10 Purl.
Rows 11–12 Rep rows 1
and 2.
Rep these 12 rows.

stripe sequences

Worked over 39 rows in stockinette stitch

A (gray) 4 rows
B (ecru) 1 row
C (blue) 9 rows
B (ecru) 2 rows
D (fawn) 2 rows
B (ecru) 1 row
D (chocolate) 4 rows
B (ecru) 2 rows
A (gray) 6 rows
B (ecru) 3 rows
D (fawn) 5 rows

Five-color Stripe

- shade of blue with earthy browns always create a popular, classic colorway

Worked over 39 rows in stockinette stitch

A (fawn) 6 rows
B and C (chocolate and blue) 1 row
A (fawn) 5 rows
C (blue) 1 row
A (fawn) 5 rows
B and C (chocolate and blue) 1 row
A (fawn) 5 rows
B and C (chocolate and blue) 1 row
A (fawn) 5 rows
B and C (chocolate and blue) 1 row
A (fawn) 5 rows
B and C (chocolate and blue) 1 row
A (fawn) 4 rows

Three-color Stripe

- this "broken" stripe variation gives vibrancy to a simple three-color layout

Five-color Stripe

- *I prefer an odd number of stripe rows, especially single-row stripes*
- *single rows are time consuming, joining in ends, but effective*

Worked over 36 rows
in stockinette stitch

A (gray) 5 rows
B (lime) 2 rows
C (ecru) 2 rows
B (lime) 2 rows
D (fawn) 1 row
E (chocolate) 1 row
D (fawn) 1 row
E (chocolate) 1 row
D (fawn) 1 row
E (chocolate) 1 row
D (fawn) 1 row
E (chocolate) 1 row
D (fawn) 1 row
E (chocolate) 1 row
D (fawn) 1 row
E (chocolate) 1 row
D (fawn) 1 row
E (chocolate) 1 row
D (fawn) 1 row
E (chocolate) 1 row
D (fawn) 1 row
B (lime) 2 rows
C (ecru) 2 rows
B (lime) 1 row
A (gray) 3 rows

Worked over 39 rows
in stockinette stitch

A (fawn) 8 rows
B (ecru) 3 rows
C (chocolate) 2 rows
B (ecru) 2 rows
D (lime) 8 rows
B (ecru) 1 row
E (gray) 3 rows
B (ecru) 2 rows
C (chocolate) 3 rows
B (ecru) 1 row
A (fawn) 2 rows
B (ecru) 1 row
D (lime) 3 rows

Multicolor Stripe

- *neutral tones work with strong brights*
- *zesty lime is one of my favorite accent colors*

project
workshops

1 Muffler

A simple yet chic little muffler knitted in the most basic stitch of all—garter stitch—which means it's the perfect first-time project. Make this scarf in a luxurious royal alpaca yarn to create a neat accessory from a refined fabric. Alternatively, experiment with other fibers, such as a hand-dyed silk, to create a pronounced textural effect and an altogether more artisan textile.

Skill level...

■□□⊃
BEGINNER

In this project you will learn...

Gauging whether there is sufficient yarn to complete a row; weaving in yarn ends for a neat finish

Stitches used...

Garter stitch

Size
Approximately 5½in/14cm wide by 37¾in/96cm long, depending on your gauge

Materials
2 x 2½oz/100g skeins (288yd/263m per skein)
   fine-weight alpaca yarn, such as
   Blue Sky Alpacas Royal 🄶🄹 FINE
or
2 x 1½oz/40g skeins (235yd/215m per skein)
   fine-weight silk yarn, such as
   Alchemy Yarns Silken Straw 🄶🄹 FINE
Pair of size 3 US (3mm) knitting needles

Gauge
28 stitches and 54 rows to 4in/10cm over garter st using 3 US (3mm) needles

To make the Muffler

Cast on 40 sts and work 37¾in/96cm in garter st (knit every row).
Bind off loosely.

To finish

Weave in any loose yarn ends. *See Masterclass, below right.*
Lay the work out flat and gently steam the finished piece.

Masterclass

Gauging whether there is sufficient yarn to complete a row

It is best not to run out of yarn in the middle of a row. If you are almost at the end of a ball of yarn and you are unsure whether you can complete the next row, lay your work flat and fold the remaining yarn back and forth over the knitting. If you have at least four times the width of your knitted piece, you will have sufficient yarn to work a row of basic stitches, such as garter or stockinette stitch. Cables, ribs, and texture stitches take more yarn.

Weaving in yarn ends for a neat finish

Whenever possible, join new balls of yarn at the beginning or end of a row. Once the project is finished, weave the loose yarn ends into either the fabric or the seams. As this garter stitch muffler is reversible, there is no "wrong side" on the fabric in which to hide the yarn ends so simply choose one side to work the ends into. Looking at the garter stitch fabric from one side, stretch it a little so that the rows spread apart—you will see one row of knitted V's alternated with one row of purl bumps. Using a large blunt-ended yarn needle threaded with the yarn end, weave it in along the row of recessed knitted V's, mimicking the path of the yarn in that row to effectively camouflage it within the fabric.

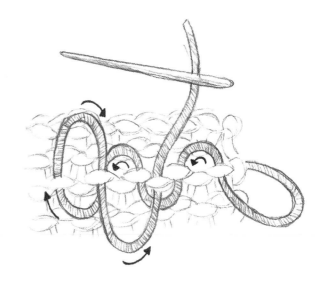

2 Dishcloth

A small knitted project to practice a basic texture stitch, which can then be put to good use as a practical, thrifty and environmentally friendly dishcloth. Knitted in unbleached natural cotton, this cloth is worked in seed stitch, which uses both knit and purl stitches alternately to create a bumpy textured, double-faced fabric. You could also work the cloth in an alternative stitch from the Stitch Library (see Masterclass, below right).

Skill level...

■□□□
BEGINNER

In this project you will learn...

Using an alternative stitch texture; reusing yarn by rewinding

Stitches used...

Moss stitch; garter stitch

Size
Approximately 8¼in/21cm wide by 10¼in/26cm long

Materials
1 x 3½oz/100g ball (197yd/180m per ball) medium-weight cotton yarn, such as Jarol King Dishcloth Cotton (4) MEDIUM
—3½oz/100g of yarn makes two cloths
Pair of size 7 US (4.5mm) knitting needles

Gauge
19 stitches and 30 rows to 4in/10cm square over seed stitch using 7 US (4.5mm) needles

To make the Dishcloth
Cast on 39 sts and work 4 rows in garter st (knit every row).
Cont in seed st as foll:
Next row * K1, p1, rep from * to last st, k1.
Rep last row until work measures 9½in/24.5cm from cast-on edge.
Work 4 rows in garter st.
Bind off.

To finish
Weave in any loose yarn ends. *See Masterclass, page 67.*
Lay the work out flat and gently steam.

Masterclass

Using an alternative stitch texture
I have used seed stitch for my dishcloth as its bumpy surface is perfect for wiping surfaces clean. Any stitch with a rough texture, such as garter stitch or purl bar stitch work equally well. *See Stitch Library, pages 50 and 54.*

Reusing yarn
Maybe you have kept a favorite sweater, much loved and worn, simply because you remember the time it took to make or the cost of the yarn. Well, provided it is not too felted, put it to good use once more. It will be washed later, so start by unpicking the seams. Find the bound-off edge and unravel each piece of knitting in turn. The yarn will be wavy, but persist. Make a hank using either a commercially available wool winder or winding the yarn around the back of a chair. Tie the hank in several places to stop it becoming tangled. Now wash the yarn. Once dry it will be straight and ready to re-use.

Fold-over Pillow

A stylish pillow created from one long piece of knitting. The open edge of the cover folds over to the front, enclosing the pillow form. Make this project in a variety of colors or textures. Here, I have paired pure silk with a mohair-blend yarn, both in stockinette stitch. Alternatively, work the covers in a different stitch using any of the pattern stitches on pages 50–51 and 54–57.

Skill level...

BEGINNER

In this project you will learn...

Achieving a neat bound-off edge; creating a neat seam using backstitch

Stitches used...

Stockinette stitch

Size
Finished size of pillow: approximately
16in/40cm square
Actual size of knitted piece:
16in/40cm wide by 55in/140cm long

Materials
4 x 1¾oz/50g balls (137yd/125m per ball) lightweight
  DK silk yarn, such as Rowan Pure Silk DK ③ LIGHT
or
8 x 1oz/25g balls (82yd/75m per ball) medium-weight
  mohair-blend yarn, such as Rowan Kid Silk Aura ④
  MEDIUM
Pair each of sizes 5 US (3.75mm) and 6 US (4mm)
  knitting needles
16in/40cm square feather pillow form

Gauge
22 stitches and 30 rows to 4in/10cm square over St st
using 6 US (4mm) needles

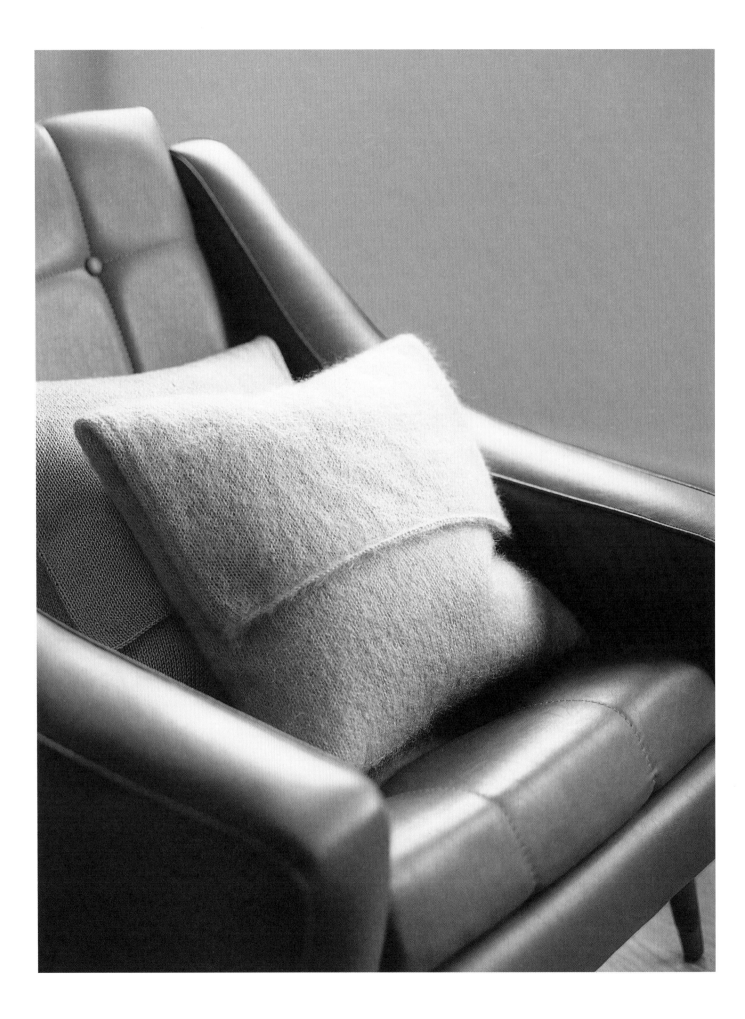

To make the Fold-over Pillow

Using 5 US (3.75mm) needles, cast on 88 sts and beg with a knit row work 6 rows in St st (knit one row and purl one row alternately).
Change to 6 US (4mm) needles and cont in St st until work measures 54¼in/138cm from cast-on edge, ending with RS facing for next row.
Change to 5 US (3.75mm) needles and work 6 rows in St st.
Bind off.

To finish

Weave in any loose yarn ends. *See Masterclass, page 67.*
Lay the work out flat and gently steam the finished piece on the reverse.
With right sides together, fold work in half widthwise and sew both side seams using backstitch. *See Masterclass, below right.*
Turn pillow cover right-side out.
Place pillow form inside cover and fold over excess fabric to front to make a flap.

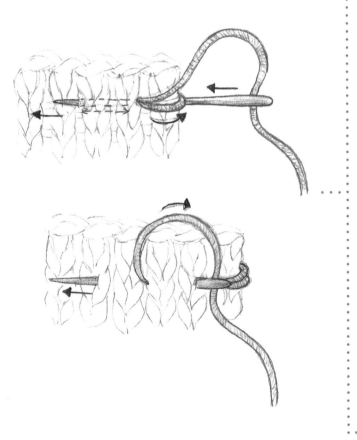

Masterclass

Achieving a neat bound-off edge

Achieving neat, even stitches across a bind-off row can be tricky. You may find that your bound-off edge is a little tighter than the rest of your knitted fabric. This can be easily remedied by using needles that are one size larger than asked for in the pattern, which will loosen the stitches and give the edge greater elasticity.

For this pillow I have cast on and bound off with a size smaller needle to deliberately create a firmer edge. Furthermore, I have bound off the stitches on a knit row so that the bound-off edge lies flat on the right side of the work and is clearly visible, giving the edge a slight roll. If you were to finish with a purlwise bind-off row, this edge would not be so visible on the right side.

Seaming using backstitch

Backstitch is the simplest and quickest way of joining together pieces of knitting. As it is worked on the wrong side, backstitch seams are not ideal when you need to match up specific stitches or patterns. However, for plain stockinette stitch, backstitch creates a good strong seam that is not too bulky.

Place the two pieces right sides together. Before you begin to sew, pin these pieces evenly along the length of the seam.

Thread a blunt-ended yarn needle with a length of yarn. Starting at the right-hand side edge, bring the needle through both layers of knitting from the back to the front approximately one stitch in from the edge. Then either take the needle back through the knitted fabric approximately one stitch back from where it first came out or take the needle around the end of the piece. Next, bring the needle back through to the front approximately one stitch in front of where you started. Pull up the yarn to tighten the stitch.

Continue along the seam, taking the needle backward and then foward through both layers of knitted fabric until you have completed the seam. Secure the end.

Notebook

This very simple notebook cover is worked in beginner's stockinette stitch with a contrasting reverse stockinette stitch spine and neat selvage edge. Filled with a selection of textural handmade papers, the notebook is sewn along the spine to secure the pages. As additional decoration, the book can be secured with a contrasting thread—leather, string, or waxed cotton—that is either tied in a bow or fastened around a button.

Skill level...

BEGINNER

In this project you will learn...

Adapting a pattern for a different yarn weight

Stitches used...

Stockinette stitch; reverse stockinette stitch

Size
Finished size of notebook: approximately 4¼in/10.5cm wide by 5½in/14cm tall by ¾in/2cm deep
Actual size of knitted piece: 9¼in/23cm wide by 5½in/14cm tall

Materials
1 x 1oz/28g ball (258yd/236m per ball) super-fine-weight cotton yarn, such as Habu Cotton Gima **1** SUPER FINE
Pair of size 2 US (2.75mm) knitting needles
or
1 x 1oz/28g ball (258yd/236m per ball) fine-weight silk yarn, such as Habu Silk Gima or Alchemy Yarns Silken Straw **2** FINE
Pair of size 3 US (3.25mm) knitting needles

Handmade paper
Hole punch
Leather thread, string, or waxed cotton thread, for optional ties
Button (optional)

Gauges
For the yarns suggested above, the gauges are as foll:
Super-fine-weight yarn: 36 stitches and 48 rows to 4in/10cm square over St st using 2 US (2.75mm) needles
Fine-weight yarn: 26 stitches and 36 rows to 4in/10cm square over St st using 3 US (3.25mm)

Masterclass

Adapting a pattern for a different yarn weight

You can use any other type of yarn to knit these notebook covers; just remember to match the size of the knitting needles you use to your choice of yarn. Knit a gauge sample and adjust the number of stitches cast on in order to make your knitted piece the size required.

This is where a calculator comes in handy. For example, to work out how many stitches you need to cast on to achieve a knitted piece with a width of 9¼ inches if you used a lightweight yarn with a gauge of 22 stitches to 4in/10cm square, divide 22 by 4 to get the number of stitches per inch—5.5. Now multiply that number by 9¼ in order to calculate the number of stitches needed to cast on to achieve the desired width of 9¼ inches—50.9. Then round that number up to the nearest whole number, so that makes 51 stitches for a knitted piece that is 9¼ inches wide.

needles

To make the Notebook cover using super-fine-weight yarn
Using 2 US (2.75mm) needles, cast on 87 sts and work as foll:
Row 1 (RS) P1, k1, p1, k1, p1, k34, p9, k34, p1, k1, p1, k1, p1.
Row 2 K1, p1, k1, p1, k1, p34, k9, p34, k1, p1, k1, p1, k1.
Rep these 2 rows until work measures 5½in/14cm, ending with RS facing for next row.
Bind off.

To make the Notebook cover using fine-weight yarn
Using 3 US (3.25mm) needles, cast on 62 sts and work as foll:
Row 1 (RS) P1, k1, p1, k25, p6, k25, p1, k1, p1.
Row 2 K1, p1, k1, p25, k6, p25, k1, p1, k1.
Rep these 2 rows until work measures 5½in/14cm, ending with RS facing for next row.
Bind off.

To finish
Weave in any loose yarn ends. *See Masterclass, page 67.*
Lay the work out flat and gently steam the finished piece on the reverse.

To make the book pages

Cut or tear selected paper or papers to the correct size for the leaves of the notebook. Alternatively, use brown wrapping or parcel paper or any other fine-weight paper folded in half to make the notebook pages.

Using a hole punch, make three evenly spaced holes along the spine edge of the gathered leaves. Slot the leaves into the knitted book jacket, leaving the neat folded edge as the visible finished edge.

To sew in the book pages

Using the same yarn as the cover, fold a long length in half to create a loop at one end. Thread a blunt-ended yarn needle with the two ends of the doubled yarn and knot at the free end. Pass the needle through the center hole [1] from front to back and secure by passing the needle through the loop and pulling up tight. Next, pass the needle through the next hole to the right [2] from front to back, then over the spine [3] and back down into the front of hole [2]. Then take the needle to the right along the back of the book, around the end of the book's spine [4] to the front and again pass it through the hole [2] from front to back.

Next, take the yarn along the back of the book's spine and through the center hole [1] from back to front.

Repeat these steps for the other end of the book. Secure with a knot.

Optional ties

Use leather thread, string, or waxed cotton thread for the optional ties. Double a long length of thread and secure it into the center hole as for sewing the book pages [1]. Secure a second doubled thread in the same way, but with the back of the book facing so that it is on the back of the book.

Next, sew a button to the center of the front of the book near the edge. Knot the end of each tie to form a buttonhole loop that can be hooked onto the button to fasten the ties.

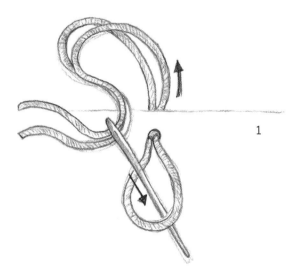

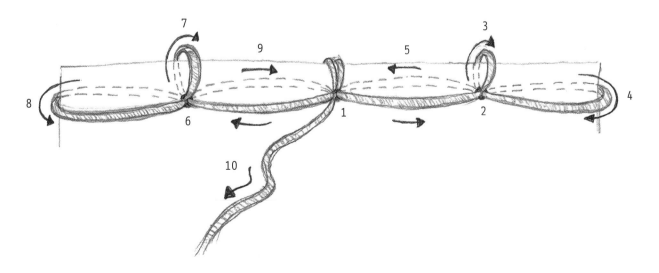

5 Shopper

This elegant bag is made up of nothing
more than one long piece of knitting
worked in bulky yarn and in a firm
double-sided stitch. The knitted strip
is then simply folded, stitched, and
finished with robust cotton webbing
tape handles to create a useful tote.

Skill level...

◖■■□□▷
EASY

In this project you will learn...

Bringing yarn to front of work, slipping stitch
purlwise, then taking yarn to back to create
tweed stitch; sewing on tape and taping a seam

Stitches used...

Tweed stitch

Size
Finished size of shopper: approximately 15in/
38cm wide by 16½in/42cm tall by 4in/10cm deep
Actual size of knitted piece: approximately
15½in/39.5cm wide tall by 41in/104cm

Materials
9 x 1¾/50g balls (46yd/42m per ball) super-bulky-
   weight wool-blend yarn, such as Debbie Bliss
   Como ⑥ SUPER BULKY
Pair of size 15 US (10mm) knitting needles
3¼yd/3m cotton tape, 1½in/3.8cm wide, for
handles
Strong sewing thread and sewing needle

Gauge
10 stitches and 15 rows to 4in/10cm square over
St st using 15 US (10mm) needles

Notes
The gauge is over St st as counting rows of tweed
stitch is tricky. If the St st gauge is correct, the

tweed stitch gauge will be correct.

To make the Shopper

The shopper is worked in one piece.
Cast on 53 sts and work in tweed stitch as foll:
Row 1 (RS) K1, * yf, sl1p, yb, k1, rep from *
to end.
Row 2 P2, * yb, sl1p, yf, p1, rep from * to
last st, p1.
Rep these 2 rows until work measures 41in/104cm
from cast-on edge, ending with RS facing for
next row.
Bind off tightly in k1, p1 rib to make a firm edge.

To finish

Weave in any loose yarn ends. *See Masterclass,
page 67.*
Lay the work out flat and gently steam the
finished piece on the reverse.
With right sides together, fold work in half
widthwise and sew both side seams using
backstitch. *See Masterclass, page 73.*
Fold approximately 2in/5cm of top edge over to
wrong side of bag and stitch in place.
To form the bag's base and gusset, with the bag
still wrong-side out, take the tips of the sewn
corners and fold inward to form a box shape (like
wrapping the ends of a parcel).
Stitch the folded corners down to the base of
the bag. Turn right-side out (with the bigger
stitch on the outside).
Cut the cotton webbing tape in half and attach to
the bag as foll:
Take one of the tape pieces and mark the center
with a pin (this is the center of the handle).
Pin the ends of the tape along the length of one
side of the bag approximately 5in/13cm apart and
so that each end of the tape ends ¾in/2cm past
the center of the bag base.
Stitch the tape in position along each side edge,
using strong sewing thread (see right).
Repeat for the handle on the other side of the
bag, overlapping the handle ends from the other
side at the base and turning the ends under.

Masterclass

Adding cotton webbing tape handles

The wide cotton twill tape applied to this
shopper not only provides the bag with robust
handles but is also a design feature. The tape
is simply attached using small whip stitches—
neat, little slanted stitches—that are evenly
spaced along the length of tape (see below).

Taping a seam

A narrow cotton twill tape or seam binding
can be used along the seams of any knitted
piece to prevent them from stretching. This
is particularly beneficial for areas such as
shoulders, which can sometimes sag and lose
their shape, as the tape stabilizes the seam.
Taping the seam can also help to ease in a
shoulder that is too wide.

Cut a piece of tape the length of the desired
shoulder width and whip stitch the tape on
either side along the shoulder seam, easing in
the fullness as desired.

This method of taping a seam is also very
useful for covering joins along neckbands and
collars, where a bulky seam may rub against
the skin and where the back neckband may
otherwise stretch out of shape (see the V-neck
on page 135 and the cardigan on page 138). I
tape the neck seam of any babies' garments in
order to protect their more delicate skin.

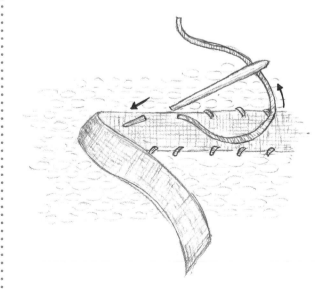

Stripe Pillow

A simple square pillow cover worked in the perennially popular stockinette stitch using a palette of complementary earthy shades, plus a shot of lime, in this five-color stripe. The back button fastening lends added decorative detail—the perfect place to start practicing how to work buttonholes.

Skill level...

EASY

In this project you will learn...

Working in stripes; making a buttonhole

Stitches used...

Stockinette stitch; k1, p1 rib

Size
Finished size of pillow: approximately 16in/40cm square
Actual size of knitted piece: 16in/40cm wide by 32in/80cm long

Materials
Double-knitting-weight linen-blend yarn, such as
Rowan Lenpur Linen **3** LIGHT
  A 1 x 1¾oz/50g ball (126yd/115m per ball) in dark gray
  B 2 x 1¾oz/50g balls (126yd/115m per ball) in off-white
  C 1 x 1¾oz/50g ball (126yd/115m per ball) in dark brown
  D 1 x 1¾oz/50g ball (126yd/115m per ball) in taupe
  E 1 x 1¾oz/50g ball (126yd/115m per ball) in lime green

Pair each of sizes 3 US (3.25mm) and 6 US (4mm) knitting needles
5 buttons, ¾in/2cm in diameter
16in/40cm square feather pillow form

Gauge
22 stitches and 30 rows to 4in/10cm square over St st using 6 US (4mm) needles

Note
Whenever you change color, it is easier to weave in any loose yarn ends as you work.
See Masterclass, page 67.

Fold along where the markers are attached, making sure the buttonhole band is on top of the button band.
Sew side seams, stitching through all layers.
Sew buttons to button band to match buttonholes.
Insert pillow form.

To make the Stripe Pillow

Using 3 US (3.25mm) needles and yarn C, cast on 88 sts and work 6 rows in k1, p1 rib as foll:
Row 1 (RS) * K1, p1, rep from * to end.
Row 2 * K1, p1, rep from * to end.
Change to yarn B and work 7 rows in k1, p1 rib as set.
Change to 6 US (4mm) needles and yarn A, beg with a knit row cont in St st (knit one row and purl one row alternately), using the stripe sequence given to **.
Note: You have already worked the first 2 stripes in the rib band and are starting the third stripe.
Change to 3 US (3.25mm) needles and yarn C, and work 5 rows in k1, p1 rib as set, ending with RS facing for next row.
Buttonhole row 1 Rib 6 sts, bind off next 3 sts, [rib until there are 15 sts on RH needle after last bind-off, bind off next 3 sts] 4 times, rib to end.
Buttonhole row 2 Change to yarn B, work across row in k1, p1 rib as set but cast on 3 sts over those bound off in previous row. *See Masterclass, opposite.*
With yarn B, work 5 rows more in k1, p1 rib.
Bind off in rib.

To finish

Weave in any loose yarn ends.
Lay the work out flat and gently steam the finished piece on the reverse.

Stripe sequence

C 6 rows
B 7 rows
A 13 rows
B 6 rows
D 6 rows
B 3 rows
E 6 rows
B 6 rows
A 6 rows
B 3 rows
C 9 rows
Place marker at each end of last row for fold line
A 4 rows
B 1 row
C 9 rows
B 4 rows
D 4 rows
B 1 row
E 16 rows
B 3 rows
C 6 rows
B 7 rows
A 13 rows
B 6 rows
D 6 rows
B 3 rows
E 6 rows
B 6 rows
A 6 rows
B 3 rows
C 9 rows
Place marker at each end of last row for fold line
A 4 rows
B 1 row
C 9 rows
B 4 rows
D 4 rows
B 1 row
E 16 rows
B 3 rows
** C 6 rows
B 7 rows

Masterclass

Making a buttonhole

There are several different types of buttonholes within knitting—horizontal, vertical, eyelet, yarn-over to name a few. I have used just one method for all the projects within this book, the horizontal buttonhole made over two rows as it is a good, all-purpose method that suits both garments and homewares alike.

Buttonholes need to be spaced evenly so that the band will not gape open when it is buttoned. Some patterns will say something like "work six buttonholes evenly spaced," but this can be tricky to work out correctly if you are having to guess how many rows between each buttonhole. For this pillow cover pattern, I have taken all the guesswork out of spacing the buttonholes by placing them horizontally along two rows.

Match your buttons to the size of the buttonhole; as knitted fabric stretches, the button should be only just able to slip through the hole. If you are in any doubt, knit a sample swatch with a buttonhole to determine whether it is the correct size. A good rule of thumb is that a buttonhole should be two stitches smaller than the width of the button.

A horizontal buttonhole is made by binding off stitches on one row and these are then offset by casting on the same number of stitches on the following row. Unless otherwise specified in the pattern, the first bind-off row of the buttonhole is worked on the right side of the piece. This is a very versatile technique as either fewer or more stitches can be bound off to vary the size of the buttonhole.

On the first row, work to the position of the buttonhole. Work two stitches and then lift the first stitch over the second one to bind off one stitch. Continue binding off the required number of stitches; for this pillow cover, it is three stitches for each buttonhole repeated at regular intervals along the row. Work to the end of the row. On the return row, work to the bound-off stitches. Turn the work and using the knit-on cast-on technique (see page 24–25), cast on the same number of stitches bound off on the previous row. Turn the work back and complete the row.

Stripe Throw

A deceptively simple throw that is worked in four easy sections, which are then pieced together. Knitted in the trinity of basic stitches—garter, stockinette, and reverse stockinette stitch—this pattern really couldn't be easier. You could knit this throw in plain block colors, but for added interest I have introduced some elementary stripe sequences of varying complexity.

Skill level...

EASY

In this project you will learn...

Putting together a simple stripe sequence; following a colorwork chart

Stitches used...

Garter stitch; stockinette stitch; reverse stockinette stitch

Size
Finished size of throw once sewn:
approximately 59in/150cm square
Actual size of each knitted piece:
approximately 29½in/75cm square

Materials
Double-knitting-weight alpaca yarn, such as
  Rowan Classic Baby Alpaca DK 〈3〉 LIGHT
  A 11 x 1¾oz/50g balls (110yd/100m per ball) in light gray
  B 9 x 1¾oz/50g balls (110yd/100m per ball) in dark gray
  C 8 x 1¾oz/50g balls (110yd/100m per ball) in brown
Pair of size 6 US (4mm) knitting needles

Gauge
22 stitches and 30 rows to 4in/10cm square over St st using 6 US (4mm) needles

Notes
Whenever you change color, it is easier to weave in any loose yarn ends as you work. *See Masterclass, page 67.*

To make the Stripe Throw
First square
Three wide stripes using yarns A, B, and C
Using yarn A, cast on 165 sts and work 2in/5cm in garter st (knit every row), ending with RS facing for next row. *You will have worked approximately 20 rows.*
Cont in St st (knit one row and purl one row alternately) with garter st edge as foll:
Row 1 (RS) Knit.
Row 2 Purl to last 12 sts, k12.
Rep last 2 rows using yarn A until work measures 10in/25cm from cast-on edge, ending with RS facing for next row. *You will have worked approximately 60 St st rows in yarn A.*
Change to yarn B and rep rows 1 and 2 until work measures 19¾in/50cm from cast-on edge, ending with RS facing for next row. *You will have worked approximately 74 St st rows in yarn B.*
Change to yarn C and rep rows 1 and 2 until work measures 29½in/75cm from cast-on edge, ending with RS facing for next row. *You will have worked approximately 74 St st rows in yarn C.*
Bind off.

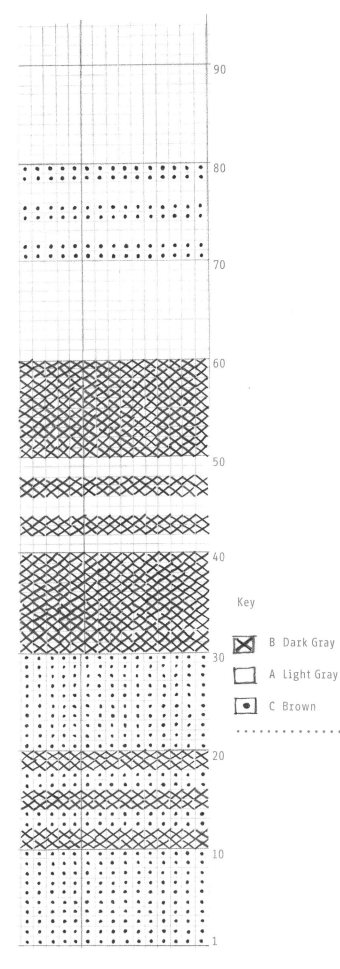

Second square
90-row stripe sequence using yarns A, B, and C
C 10 rows
B 2 rows
C 2 rows
B 2 rows
C 2 rows
B 2 rows
C 10 rows
B 10 rows
A 2 rows
B 2 rows
A 2 rows
B 2 rows
A 2 rows
B 10 rows
A 10 rows
C 2 rows
A 2 rows
C 2 rows
A 2 rows
C 2 rows
A 10 rows

Using yarn B, cast on 165 sts and work 2in/5cm in garter st, ending with RS facing for next row. *You will have worked approximately 20 rows.*
Cont in St st with garter st edge, changing color as given in stripe sequence above or shown in the chart left, as foll:

Key

⊠ B Dark Gray

☐ A Light Gray

⊡ C Brown

Masterclass

How to read a colorwork chart
Colorwork instructions can either be written out in full within the knitting pattern or represented as a chart on graph paper. The different shades of yarn that make up the colorwork motif are represented either as a shaded color (see page 46) or, as shown here, as a symbol.

With both types of colorwork chart, each square of the chart represents one stitch, and each line of squares represents one row. The right-side rows (or odd-numbered knit rows) are read from right to left, while the wrong-side rows (or even-numbered purl rows) are read from left to right. The rows of the chart are read from the bottom to the top.

** Row 1 (RS) Knit.
Row 2 Purl to last 12 sts, k12. **
Rep last 2 rows, keeping color sequence correct, until work measures 29½in/75cm from cast-on edge, ending with RS facing for next row.
Bind off.

Third square
16-row stripe repeat using yarns A, B, and C
Stripe repeat to be worked throughout:
C 3 rows
B 1 row
C 3 rows
A 9 rows

Using yarn C, cast on 165 sts and work 2in/5cm in garter st ending with RS facing for next row. *You will have worked approximately 20 rows.*
Cont in St st with garter st edge, changing color as given in stripe sequence above, as foll:
Rep as for Second Square from ** to **.
Rep last 2 rows, keeping color sequence correct, until work measures 29½in/75cm from cast-on edge, ending with RS facing for next row.
Bind off.

Fourth square
Four-row stripe repeat using yarns A and B
Stripe repeat to be worked throughout:
A 2 rows
B 2 rows

Using yarn A, cast on 165 sts and work 2in/5cm in garter st changing color as given in stripe sequence above, ending with RS facing for next row. *You will have worked approximately 20 rows.*
Cont in St st with garter st edge, keeping color sequence correct, as foll:
Rep as for Second Square from ** to **.
Rep last 2 rows, keeping color sequence correct, until work measures 15¼in/39cm from cast-on edge, ending with RS facing for next row.
Keeping color sequence correct, cont in rev St st as foll:
Row 1 (RS) K12, purl to end.
Row 2 Knit.
Rep last 2 rows, keeping color sequence correct, until work measures 29½in/75cm from cast-on edge, ending with RS facing for next row.
Bind off.

To finish
Weave in any loose yarn ends. *See Masterclass, page 67.*
Lay the work out flat and gently steam the finished piece on the reverse.
Sew the bound-off edge of the first square to the left selvage of the fourth square.
Sew the bound-off edge of the third square to the left selvage of the second square.
Sew these two strips together down the center, as shown in the diagram below. *The arrows show the direction of the knitting, with the cast-on edge at the base and the bound-off edge at the tip of the arrow.*

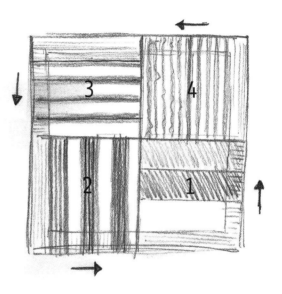

Pull-on Hats

Two essential winter hats—one plain beanie in stockinette stitch with a roll edge, the other a basic "New Yorker" style in simple k1, p1 rib. Both hats are made in luxurious alpaca yarns for maximum softness, comfort, and warmth. These hats are easy to make with small amounts of decreasing so they are a great introduction to easy shaping techniques.

Skill level...

EASY

In this project you will learn...

Working simple shaping using decreases

Stitches used...

Stockinette stitch; k1, p1 rib; k2, p2 rib

Size

One size to fit average adult head

For the plain hat

Materials

2 x 3½oz/100g skeins (100yd/91m per skein) of medium-weight alpaca-blend yarn, such as Blue Sky Alpacas Worsted Hand Dyes (4) MEDIUM
Pair of size 9 US (5.5mm) knitting needles

Gauge

16 sts and 22 rows to 4in/10cm square over St st using 9 US (5.5mm) needles

For the rib hat

Materials

1 x 3½oz/100g skein (288yd/263m per skein) of fine-weight alpaca yarn, such as Blue Sky Alpacas Royal (2) FINE
Pair of size 6 US (4mm) knitting needles

Gauge

22 stitches and 30 rows to 4in/10cm square over St st using 6 US (4mm) needles

To knit the plain hat

Cast on 78 sts and beg with a knit row, work 38 rows in St st (knit one row and purl one row alternately), ending with RS facing for next row.

Shape crown

Row 1 (RS) K8, [k2tog tbl, k1, k2tog, k14] 3 times, k2tog tbl, k1, k2tog, k8.
70 sts.

Row 2 and all WS rows Purl.

Row 3 K7, [k2tog tbl, k1, k2tog, k12] 3 times, k2tog tbl, k1, k2tog, k7.
62 sts.

Row 5 K6, [k2tog tbl, k1, k2tog, k10] 3 times, k2tog tbl, k1, k2tog, k6.
54 sts.

Row 7 K5, [k2tog tbl, k1, k2tog, k8] 3 times, k2tog tbl, k1, k2tog, k5.
46 sts.

Row 9 K4, [k2tog tbl, k1, k2tog, k6] 3 times, k2tog tbl, k1, k2tog, k4.
38 sts.

Row 11 K3, [k2tog tbl, k1, k2tog, k4] 3 times, k2tog tbl, k1, k2tog, k3.
30 sts.

Row 13 K2, [k2tog tbl, k1, k2tog, k2] 3 times, k2tog tbl, k1, k2tog, k2.
22 sts.

Row 15 K1, [k2tog tbl, k1, k2tog] 4 times, k1.
14 sts.

Cut working yarn, leaving a long end. Thread yarn end through remaining stitches, pull tight, and secure.

To knit the rib hat

Cast on 112 sts and work in k2, p2 rib until work measures 10in/25cm from cast-on edge.

Shape crown

Next row (RS) [K2tog tbl, p2tog] to end.
56 sts.

Work 5 rows in k1, p1 rib.

Next row [K2tog tbl] to end.
28 sts.

Purl 1 row.

Next row [K2tog tbl] to end.
14 sts.

Cut working yarn, leaving a long end. Thread yarn end through remaining stitches, pull tight, and secure.

To finish

Weave in any loose yarn ends. *See Masterclass, page 67.*

Lay the work out flat and gently steam the reverse side of the finished piece, taking care not to flatten the rib.

Sew the back seam using mattress stitch. *See Masterclass, pages 40 and 41.*

Masterclass

Simple shaping

The shaping of the crown for both these hats uses nothing more than the simplest method of decreasing—knitting two stitches together, so where you previously had two stitches on the needle, you now have only one.

Whenever I am designing, to keep it simple I make sure that all the decreasing is done on a right-side row. And preferably on a knit stitch, as most knitters find it easier to work a knit 2 together than a purl 2 together, especially when it comes to working through the back loops. (See pages 30–31.)

Whether you work through the front or back loops determines which direction the resulting stitch will slant toward. I like to incorporate such details into my designs, making it a feature. This is commonly known as fully fashioned shaping—we'll come back to this later on with the woman's V-neck and cardigan on pages 134–41.

9 Rag Bag

A useful bag made from strips of shirting fabric—either store-bought remnants or charity or thrift store shirts—which are cut into strips, knotted, and knitted up in simple stockinette stitch to create a circular bag with integral handles. As well as handling a less familiar knitting medium, with this bag project you will be mastering basic increasing. For ease and a neater finish, in my designs I always work the increase or decrease rows on a knit side.

Skill level...

■■□□□
EASY

In this project you will learn...

Creating and knitting with unusual yarns; increasing once knitwise

Stitches used...

Stockinette stitch

Size
Finished size of bag: approximately 13¾in/35cm tall (including handle) by 12½in/32cm in diameter
Actual size of knitted piece: approximately 18in/46cm tall (excluding handle) by 33½in/85cm wide

Materials
50 x 59in/1.5m cut lengths of lightweight cotton fabric, each strip 1in/2.5cm wide 🄶 SUPER BULKY
Pair of size 15 US (10mm) knitting needles

Gauge
9 stitches and 12 rows to 4in/10cm square over St st using 15 US (10mm) needles

Masterclass

Making your own yarn from fabric
Knitting can be made up of any continuous length of yarn, and that includes strips of shirting fabric as used here. In the past I have used many different materials, even strips cut from plastic shopping bags.

Starting at one corner of the fabric, cut along one side 1in/2.5cm in from the edge, but stopping when you are 1in/2.5cm from the end. Next, make another cut in the opposite direction, 1in/2.5cm from the previous cut and again stopping before you reach the end of the fabric. Continue making cuts in this way across the whole surface of the fabric. This will make one continuous 1in/2.5cm wide length of fabric in a sort of spiral. Knot all the lengths of fabric together and wind into a ball. Now it is ready to be knitted up.

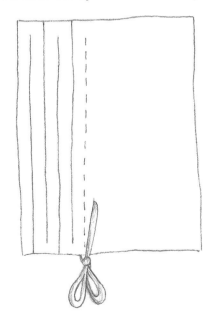

Masterclass

Increasing one stitch knitwise

This increase is sometimes called a bar increase and is made by knitting into both the front and back of a single stitch.

Work to the position of the increase. Insert the right-hand needle knitwise into the next stitch. Wrap the yarn counterclockwise around the needle and pull it through as though knitting, but leave the stitch on the left-hand needle.

Next, insert the right-hand needle into the back of the same stitch, wrap the yarn counterclockwise around the needle and pull it through. Slip the original stitch off the left-hand needle. This adds one extra stitch.

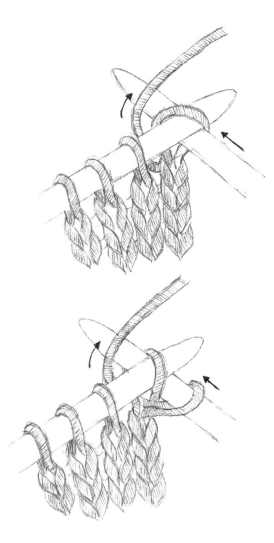

To make the Rag Bag
Cast on 5 sts.
Row 1 (RS) [Inc knitwise in next stitch] 4 times, k1.
9 sts.
Rows 2, 4, 6, 8, 10, 12, 14, and 16 Purl.
Row 3 [Inc knitwise in next stitch] 8 times, k1.
17 sts.
Row 5 [K1, inc in next stitch] 8 times, k1.
25 sts.
Row 7 [K2, inc in next stitch] 8 times, k1.
33 sts.
Row 9 [K3, inc in next stitch] 8 times, k1.
41 sts.
Row 11 [K4, inc in next stitch] 8 times, k1.
49 sts.
Row 13 [K5, inc in next stitch] 8 times, k1.
57 sts.
Row 15 [K6, inc in next stitch] 8 times, k1.
65 sts.
Row 17 [K7, inc in next stitch] 8 times, k1.
73 sts.
Row 18 (WS) Knit. *This row makes a ridge on RS of fabric.*
Beg with a knit row, cont in St st (knit one row and purl one row alternately) until work measures 13¾in/35cm from the ridge, ending with RS facing for next row.
Work handles as foll:
Next row K12, bind off next 14 sts, knit until there are 21 sts on RH needle after bind-off, bind off next 14 sts, knit to end.
Next row Purl and cast on 28 sts over each set of 14 sts bound off in previous row.
101 sts.
Next row Knit.
Next row Purl.
Bind off.

To finish
Weave in any loose yarn ends. *See Masterclass, page 67.*
Lay the work out flat and gently steam the reverse side of the finished piece.
Sew the back seam using mattress stitch. *See Masterclass, page 40.*

Mittens

Practical mittens made in k2, p1 rib and stockinette stitch with a shaped thumb and simple bound-off edge finish. Made in a natural rare sheeps breed wool with a generous rib cuff, which can either be turned down for a wrist-length mitten or kept up to extend way past the wrist so there's no gap between coat sleeve and mitten!

Skill level...

EASY

In this project you will learn...
Increasing twice knitwise

Stitches used...
Stockinette stitch; k2, p1 rib

Size
One size to fit woman's average-size hand

Materials
2 x 1¾oz/50g balls (131yd/120m per ball) of double-knitting-weight wool yarn, such as Rowan British Sheeps Breed DK **3** LIGHT
Pair each of sizes 6 US (4mm) and 7 US (4.5mm) knitting needles

Gauge
22 stitches and 30 rows to 4in/10cm square over St st using 6 US (4mm) needles

To knit the Mittens
Right mitten
Using 7 US (4.5mm) needles, cast on 44 sts and work in rib as foll:
Row 1 (RS) * K2, p1, rep from * to last 2 sts, k2.
Row 2 P2, * k1, p2, rep from * to end.
Rep last 2 rows until work measures 5in/13cm from cast-on edge, ending with RS facing for next row.
Change to 6 US (4mm) needles and cont in rib as set until work measures 9½in/24cm from cast-on edge, ending with RS facing for next row.
Cont in St st (knit one row and purl one row alternately) as foll:
Shape thumb gusset
Row 1 (inc row) K22, inc knitwise into next stitch, k1, inc knitwise into next stitch, k19. *46 sts.*
Row 2 Purl.
Row 3 Knit.
Row 4 Purl.
Row 5 (inc row) K22, inc knitwise into next stitch, k3, inc knitwise into next stitch, k19. *48 sts.*
Cont to inc 1 st on each side of thumb gusset on every 4th row until there are 56 sts.
Work 1 row without shaping.
Next row K37, turn.
Next row Inc twice knitwise into next stitch, p15, turn.

Next row Inc twice knitwise into next stitch, k to end of row.
18 sts.
** Beg with a purl row, work 7 rows in St st.
Bind off.
Cut working yarn, leaving a long end. *You will use this yarn end to sew up the thumb seam.*
With RS facing, rejoin yarn and using RH needle, pick up and knit 4 sts at base of thumb, knit to end of row.
46 sts.
Beg with a purl row work 17 rows in St st, ending with RS facing for next row.
Bind off. **

Left Mitten
Work to match Right Mitten, reversing position of thumb gusset as foll:
Shape thumb gusset
Row 1 (inc row) K19, inc knitwise into next stitch, k1, inc knitwise into next stitch, k22.
46 sts.
Row 2 Purl.
Row 3 Knit.
Row 4 Purl.
Row 5 (inc row) K19, inc knitwise into next stitch, k3, inc knitwise into next stitch, k22.
Cont to inc 1 st at each side of thumb gusset on every 4th row until there are 56 sts.
Work 1 row without shaping.
Next row K34, turn.
Next row Inc twice knitwise into next stitch, p15, turn.
Next row Inc twice knitwise into next stitch, k to end.
18 sts.
Complete as given for Right Mitten from ** to **.

To finish
Weave in any loose yarn ends. *See Masterclass, page 67.*
Lay the work out flat and gently steam the reverse side of the finished piece, taking care not to flatten the rib.
Sew the side seam using mattress stitch.
See Masterclass, pages 40 and 41.

Masterclass

Increasing twice knitwise

Occasionally, within a row you will need to increase by more than one stitch at a time, such as when knitting the thumb gusset of these mittens. Increasing twice knitwise is worked using exactly the same principle as when you are increasing once knitwise but obviously you end up with more stitches.

Work to the position of the increase. Insert the right-hand needle knitwise into the front of the stitch to be increased. Wrap the yarn counterclockwise around the needle and pull it through as if knitting, but leave the stitch on the left-hand needle.

Insert the right-hand needle into the back of the same stitch on the left-hand needle. Wrap the yarn counterclockwise around the needle and pull it through.

Knit into the front of the same stitch as before. Then slip the original stitch from the left-hand needle. You now have three stitches on the right-hand needle.

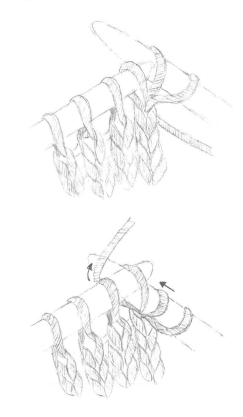

Round Pillow

This deceptively simple round pillow, made in timeless linen yarn and finished with natural horn buttons, uses a technique called short row shaping. Before completing a full row of stitches, you turn, wrap the end stitch, and continue in the opposite direction, hence the term short row. Some designers hide the wraps made at each turning point, however, I love the effect they give and prefer to incorporate them into the design.

Skill level...

INTERMEDIATE

In this project you will learn...

Short-row shaping

Stitches used...

Stockinette stitch

Size
Finished size of pillow: approximately 15in/38cm in diameter by 3¼in/8cm deep
Actual size of knitted piece: approximately 17¼in/44cm in diameter

Materials
3 x 1¾/50g balls (126yd/115m per ball) of double-knitting-weight linen-blend yarn, such as Rowan Lenpur Linen **③ LIGHT**
Pair of size 6 US (4mm) knitting needles
16in/40cm diameter round feather pillow form
2 four-hole buttons, 1in/2.5cm in diameter

Gauge
22 stitches and 30 rows to 4in/10cm square over St st using 6 US (4mm) needles

To make the Round Pillow
Front
Cast on 44 sts.
Work in St st (knit one row and purl one row alternately) and short rows as foll:
Row 1 Knit to end.
Row 2 Purl to end.
Row 3 Knit 42 sts, wrap next stitch, turn.
See Masterclass on short-row shaping, page 104.
Row 4 Purl to end.
Row 5 Knit 40 sts, wrap next stitch, turn.
Row 6 Purl to end.
Cont working in short rows as set, leaving 2 sts more unworked on every knit row until there are no more sts to knit.
This completes the first segment of the circle.
Beg again with Row 1 and cont until 8 segments have been worked to form a full circle.
Do not bind off sts, but join last segment to first segment by grafting one stitch from the needle with the corresponding stitch on the cast-on edge. *See pages 41 and 113.*

Back
Make exactly as for Front.

To finish
Weave in any loose yarn ends. *See Masterclass, page 67.*
Lay the work out flat and gently steam the finished pieces on the reverse.
Sew the two pieces together around the curved edges using backstitch and leaving an opening for inserting the pillow form.
Insert the pillow form and neatly sew the opening closed.
Take a thread and gently gather together the small hole in the center of both the Front and the Back. Sew a button to both the Front and the Back of the pillow at the same time, stitching through all the layers.

Masterclass

Short-row shaping

Short rows are partial rows of knitting that create a curve or other shape. The result is that one side or section has more rows that the other, but no stitches are decreased. This technique is sometimes called "turning" because the work is turned within the row. Short rows can be worked on one or both sides of a piece at the same time. Shaping with short rows creates a smoother shape and eliminates the jagged edges that occur when you bind off a series of stitches such as at shoulder or on collars.

When the instructions for any row say "turn," this means that the remaining stitches are not worked. To avoid creating a hole when turning on a knit row, work a wrap stitch as follows:

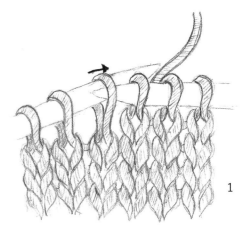

Wrapping a knit stitch

1 Work up to the "turn." With the yarn at the back of the work, slip the next stitch purlwise onto the right-hand needle.
2 Bring the yarn to the front of the work between the two needles.
3 Slip the same stitch back onto the left-hand needle and return the yarn to the back of the work between the two needles. Turn the work. One stitch is wrapped and you are ready to continue the next row.

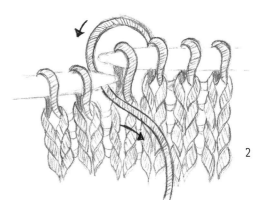

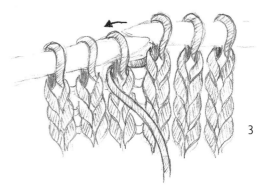

Two-needle Socks

An introduction to knitting socks—something every new knitter should try to master. Cozy and comfortable, these chunky socks are the perfect accompaniment for the now classic slipper-boot. Using basic k1, p1 rib and stockinette stitch, short row shaping forms the heel while fully fashioned decreasing gives a professional finish to the toe.

Skill level...

INTERMEDIATE

In this project you will learn...

Fully fashioned shaping; short-row shaping

Stitches used...

Stockinette stitch; k1, p1 rib

Size
Finished size of socks: to fit women's average shoe size 6.5–9.5 (see Note below)
Actual size of knitted piece:
16in/40cm tall by 8¼in/21cm wide

Materials
3 x 1¾oz/50g balls (95yd/87m per ball) of aran-weight wool-blend yarn, such as Rowan Cashsoft Aran **4** MEDIUM
Pair each of sizes 7 US (4.5mm) and 8 US (5mm) knitting needles

Gauge
19 stitches and 25 rows to 4in/10cm square over St st using 7 US (4.5mm) needles

Note
You can adjust the length of the sock to make it suitable for either a smaller or larger shoe size by working more or fewer rows right after the heel shaping.

Masterclass

Fully fashioned shaping
Fully fashioning is a technique whereby the increase and decrease stitches for the shaping within the knitting are used deliberately for decorative effect, as seen in the toe of this simple sock. Both increase and decrease stitches slope in certain directions, so this can be incorporated as an integral part of a design. When working fully fashioned shaping on garments (see pages 134–141), the increases and decreases are usually worked three stitches in from the edges of the knitting so that they are visible once the piece has been seamed.

To increase at each end of a knit row:
K3, make 1 stitch by picking up the horizontal loop before the next stitch and working into the back of it, k to last 3 sts, make 1 st as before, k3.

To decrease at each end of a knit row:
K3, k2tog, k to last 5 sts, k2tog tbl, k3.

To decrease at each end of a purl row:
P3, p2tog tbl, p to last 5 sts, p2tog, p3.

To make the Two-needle Socks

First sock

Using 8 US (5mm) needles, cast on 40 sts and work 2½in/6.5cm in knit 1, purl 1 rib.

Change to 7 US (4.5mm) needles and cont in rib as set until work measures 5in/12.5cm from cast-on edge.

Beg with a knit row, work in St st (knit one row and purl one row alternately) until work measures 7¾in/19.5cm from cast-on edge, ending with RS facing for next row.

Shape heel

Row 1 (RS) K13, wrap next stitch, turn.

See Masterclass on short-row shaping, page 105.

Row 2 and all following WS rows Purl.

Row 3 K12, wrap next stitch, turn.

Row 5 K11, wrap next stitch, turn.

Row 7 K10, wrap next stitch, turn.

Row 9 K9, wrap next stitch, turn.

Row 11 K8, wrap next stitch, turn.

Row 13 K7, wrap next stitch, turn.

Row 15 K6, wrap next stitch, turn.

Row 17 K5, wrap next stitch, turn.

Row 19 K6, wrap next stitch, turn.

Row 21 K7, wrap next stitch, turn.

Row 23 K8, wrap next stitch, turn.

Row 25 K9, wrap next stitch, turn.

Row 27 K10, wrap next stitch, turn.

Row 29 K11, wrap next stitch, turn.

Row 31 K12, wrap next stitch, turn.

Row 33 K13, wrap next stitch, turn.

Row 35 Knit across ALL stitches.

Row 36 P13, wrap next stitch, turn.

Row 37 and all foll RS rows Knit.

Row 38 P12, wrap next stitch, turn.

Row 40 P11, wrap next stitch, turn.

Row 42 P10, wrap next stitch, turn.

Row 44 P9, wrap next stitch, turn.

Row 46 P8, wrap next stitch, turn.

Row 48 P7, wrap next stitch, turn.

Row 50 P6, wrap next stitch, turn.

Row 52 P5, wrap next stitch, turn.

Row 54 P6, wrap next stitch, turn.

Row 56 P7, wrap next stitch, turn.

Row 58 P8, wrap next stitch, turn.

Row 60 P9, wrap next stitch, turn.

Row 62 P10, wrap next stitch, turn.

Row 64 P11, wrap next stitch, turn.

Row 66 P12, wrap next stitch, turn.

Row 68 P13, wrap next stitch, turn.

Row 70 Purl across ALL stitches and place marker at each end of row.

Beg with a knit row, cont in St st until work measures 5in/12.5cm from markers, ending with RS facing for next row.

Adjust the length of sock here by working more or fewer rows without shaping.

Shape toe

Row 1 (RS) K7, k2tog, k2, k2tog tbl, k14, k2tog, k2, k2tog tbl, k7.

36 sts.

Row 2 and all following WS rows Purl.

Row 3 K6, k2tog, k2, k2tog tbl, k12, k2tog, k2, k2tog tbl, k6.

32 sts.

Row 5 K5, k2tog, k2, k2tog tbl, k10, k2tog, k2, k2tog tbl, k5.

28 sts.

Row 7 K4, k2tog, k2, k2tog tbl, k8, k2tog, k2, k2tog tbl, k4.

24 sts.

Row 9 K3, k2tog, k2, k2tog tbl, k6, k2tog, k2, k2tog tbl, k3.

20 sts.

Row 11 K2, k2tog, k2, k2tog tbl, k4, k2tog, k2, k2tog tbl, k2.

16 sts.

Row 12 Purl.

Bind off.

Second sock

Make second sock in exactly same way as first.

To finish

Weave in any loose yarn ends. *See Masterclass, page 67.*

Lay the work out flat and gently steam the reverse side of the finished piece, taking care not to flatten the rib.

Starting at the toe, sew the long seam using mattress stitch (see pages 40 and 41) but reversing the seam at the turnover part of the rib (the section worked on the larger needles).

Overcast stitch the toe seam on the right side.

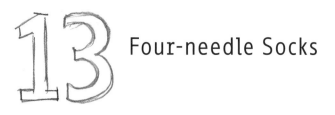

Four-needle Socks

A classic pair of stripey socks in six sizes, worked on four needles. These socks are much easier to knit than they look as the yarn is a fine self-striping wool, so there is no need for any tricky color changes. This design is finished using Kitchener stitch to give a neat, flat toe and very professional finish.

Skill level...

EXPERIENCED

In this project you will learn...

Knitting in the round on four needles; finishing a sock toe with Kitchener stitch

Stitches used...

Stockinette stitch; k1, p1 rib

Sizes

1st	2nd	3rd	4th	5th	6th

To fit childrens' shoe sizes
7¹/2–9¹/2 10¹/2–13¹/2

To fit women's shoe sizes
3–5¹/2   6–8¹/2   9–11   11¹/2–14

To fit men's shoe sizes
2–4¹/2   5–7¹/2   8–10   10¹/2–13

Materials

2 (2: 2: 2: 2: 2) x 1¾oz/50g balls (126yd/115m per ball) of 4ply wool-blend yarn, such as Regia 4-Ply Erika Knight Design Line Sock Yarn
  SUPER FINE
Set of four size 2 US (2.75mm) double-pointed needles
Stitch marker

Gauge

30 stitches and 42 rows to 4in/10cm square over St st using 2 US (2.75mm) needles

To make the Four-needle Socks

First sock

Cast on 48 (52: 56: 60: 64: 68) sts.

Divide stitches between three needles and join by sliding last stitch onto same needles as first.

Slide a stitch marker onto the needle to mark beginning of round.

Rib cuff

Round 1 [K1, p1] rep to end.

Rep Round 1 until work measures 6 (6¼: 6¾: 7: 7½: 8)in/15 (16: 17: 18: 19: 20)cm.

Heel flap

K12, (13: 14: 15: 16: 17), turn.

Row 1 Sl1p, p23 (25: 27: 29: 31: 33), turn.

24 (26: 28: 30: 32: 34) sts on this needle.

Slide rem sts onto spare needle.

Row 2 Sl1k, k23 (25: 27: 29: 31: 33), turn.

Working back and forth on these 24 (26: 28: 30: 32: 34) sts, rep last two rows 10 (11: 12: 13: 14: 15) times more.

Heel shaping

Row 1 Sl1p, p12 (14: 16: 16: 18: 18), p2tog, p1, turn.

Row 2 Sl1k, k3 (5: 6: 5: 6: 5), k2tog tbl, k1, turn.

Row 3 Sl1p, p4 (6: 7: 6: 7: 6), p2tog, p1, turn.

Row 4 Sl1k, k5 (7: 8: 7: 8: 7), k2tog tbl, k1, turn.

Cont in this manner, taking in one more stitch each row as set, until all the heel flap stitches have been included.

Pick up for instep

Pick up and knit 12 (13: 14: 15: 16: 17) sts down side of heel flap, k24 (26: 28: 30: 32: 34) sts from cuff, pick up and knit 12 (13: 14: 15: 16: 17) sts up side of heel flap, k7 (8: 9: 9: 10: 10). *62 (68: 74: 78: 84: 88) sts ending at marker.*

Shape instep

Round 1 K17 (19: 21: 22: 24: 25), k2tog, k24 (26: 28: 30: 32: 34), k2tog tbl, knit to end. *60 (66: 72: 76: 82: 86) sts.*

Round 2 Knit to end of round.

Round 3 K16 (18: 20: 21: 23: 24), k2tog, k24 (26: 28: 30: 32: 34), k2tog tbl, knit to end. *58 (64: 70: 74: 80: 84) sts.*

Round 4 Knit to end of round.

Cont in this manner, dec 2 sts on every alt row as set, until 48 (52: 56: 60: 64: 68) sts rem.

Foot

Next round Knit to end of round.

Rep this round until foot measures 5½ (6¼: 7: 8: 8¾: 9¾)in/14 (16: 18: 20: 22.5: 24.5)cm from back of heel.

Decrease for toe

Round 1 K9 (10: 11: 12: 13: 14), k2tog, k2, k2tog tbl, k18 (20: 22: 24: 26: 28), k2tog, k2, k2tog tbl, knit to end of round.

Round 2 Knit to end of round.

Round 3 K8 (9: 10: 11: 12: 13), k2tog, k2, k2tog tbl, k16 (18: 20: 22: 24: 26), k2tog, k2, k2tog tbl, knit to end of round.

Round 4 Knit to end of round.

Cont in this manner, dec 4 sts on every alt round as set, until 24 (28: 28: 32: 32: 36) sts rem.

Next round K18 (21: 21: 24: 24: 27).

Rearrange stitches so first 6 (7: 7: 8: 8: 9) sts and last 6 (7: 7: 8: 8: 9) sts of round are on one needle with the remaining 12 (14: 14: 16: 16: 18) sts on another needle.

Finish sock as explained below.

Second sock

Make second sock in exactly same way as first.

To finish

Graft toe together using Kitchener stitch. *See Masterclass, opposite.*

Weave in any loose yarn ends. *See Masterclass, page 67.*

Lay the work out flat and gently steam the reverse side of the finished piece, taking care not to flatten the rib.

Masterclass

Grafting a sock toe using Kitchener stitch

Cut the working yarn leaving a 12in/30cm tail. Thread through a tapestry needle.

Hold the two remaining knitting needles together, parallel to one another, with the knitting needle from which the long tail comes from at the back.

1 * Insert the tapestry needle purlwise into the first stitch on the front knitting needle. Pull the yarn through, leaving the stitch on the knitting needle.
2 Insert the tapestry needle knitwise into the first stitch on the back knitting needle. Pull the yarn through, leaving the stitch on the knitting needle.
3 Insert the tapestry needle knitwise into the first stitch on the front needle and slip the stitch off the needle.
4 Insert the tapestry needle purlwise into the next stitch on the front needle. Pull the yarn through, leaving the stitch on the needle.
5 Insert the tapestry needle purlwise into the first stitch on the back needle and slip the stitch off the needle.
6 Insert the tapestry needle knitwise into the next stitch on the back needle. Pull the yarn through, leaving the stitch on the needle.
Repeat from * until all the stitches have been grafted. Secure the yarn end on the inside of the sock.

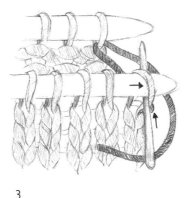

1

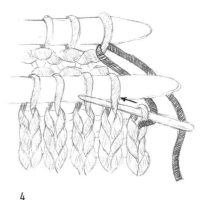

2

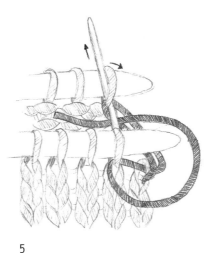

3

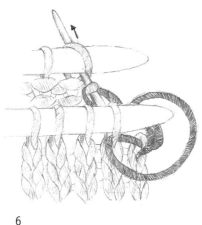

4

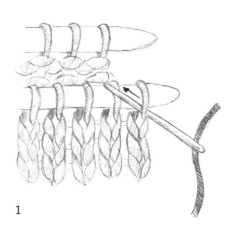

5

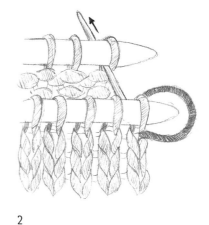

6

 Cable Scarf

A long, long scarf knitted in super-bulky yarn worked on super-fat knitting needles, this design incorporates an oversized cable stitch with a neat selvage edge. It is the perfect project for a novice to try out cables because by working in such thick yarn on large needles the cable stitches are clearly visible, so you will be able to see the cable taking shape as you knit.

Skill level...

EXPERIENCED

In this project you will learn...
How to work a cable

Stitches used...
Stockinette stitch; reverse stockinette stitch; cable C12B

Size
Approximately 9in/23cm wide by 90in/230cm long, depending on your gauge

Materials
5 x 3½oz/100g balls (87yd/80m per ball) of super-bulky-weight wool yarn, such as Rowan Big Wool **(6)** SUPER BULKY
Pair of size 17 US (12mm) knitting needles
Cable needle

Gauge
9 stitches and 12 rows to 4in/10cm square over St st using 17 US (12mm) needles

Special abbreviation
C12B cable 12 back—slip next 6 sts onto cable needle and hold at back of work, k6 from LH needle, then k6 from cable needle

To make the Cable scarf
Cast on 26 sts and work in rib as foll:
Rib row 1 (RS) [K2, p1] to last 2 sts, k2.
Rib row 2 [P2, k1] to last 2 sts, p2.
Rep last 2 rows until work measures 9in/23cm, ending with RS facing for next row.
Now work in cable patt as foll:
Row 1 (RS) K2, p5, k12, p5, k2.
Row 2 P2, k5, p12, k5, p2.
Row 3 K2, p5, C12B, p5, k2.
Row 4 Rep row 2.
Rows 5–16 [Rep rows 1 and 2] 6 times.
Rep these 16 rows 11 times more, then work rows 1–6, ending with RS facing for next row.
Rep rib rows 1 and 2 until rib measures 9in/23cm, ending with RS facing for next row.
Bind off in rib.

To finish
Weave in any loose yarn ends. *See Masterclass, page 67.*
Lay the work out flat and gently steam the finished piece on the reverse.

Masterclass

How to knit a cable

Cables are made by crossing groups of stitches within a row using a third short needle, known as a cable needle. Originating from the islands of Scotland, they are a traditional form of decorative knitting known as Aran. While it may look complex, cabling is actually deceptively simple. The cabling technique shown here can be done with any number of stitches, such as in the Cable Hot-water Bottle Cover on pages 118–21 where it is worked over 8 stitches instead of 12. Holding the cable needle to the back of the work makes a cable that twists to the right. To make a cable that twists to the left, simply hold the cable needle to the front of the work.

Cable 12 back (C12B)

Work to the position of the cable. Slip the first six cable stitches purlwise off the left-hand needle and onto the cable needle. Leave the cable needle at the back of the work, then knit the next six stitches on the left-hand needle, keeping the yarn tight to prevent a gap forming in the knitting. Knit the six stitches directly from the cable needle, or if preferred, slip the six stitches from the cable needle back onto the left-hand needle and then knit them. This completes the cable cross.

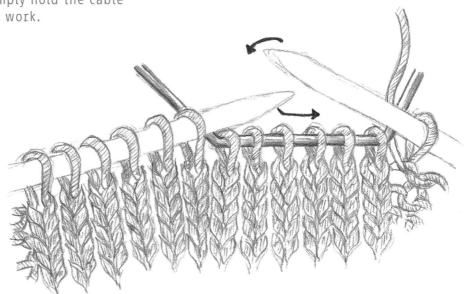

Cable Hot-water Bottle Cover

Dress up your hot-water bottle with this elegant yet practical knitted cover. Made in soft, natural cotton, the stylish cable plait stitch design is finished with a contrasting rib turtleneck.

Skill level...

■■■□

INTERMEDIATE

In this project you will learn...

Working a cable braid

Stitches used...

Reverse stockinette stitch; k1, p1 rib; cable braid stitch

Size
One size to fit average size hot-water bottle
Actual size of knitted piece: 8in/20cm wide by 13in/33cm long

Materials
3 x 1¾oz/50g balls (98yd/90m per ball) medium-weight cotton yarn, such as Debbie Bliss Eco Fairtrade Cotton (4) MEDIUM
Pair each of sizes 6 US (4mm) and 7 US (4.5mm) knitting needles
Size 7 US (4.5mm) cable needle

Gauge
18 stitches and 24 rows to 4in/10cm square over St st using 7 US (4.5mm) needles

Special abbreviations
C8F cable 8 front—slip next 4 sts onto cable needle and hold at front of work, k4 from LH needle, then k4 from cable needle.
C8B cable 8 back—slip next 4 sts onto cable needle and hold at back of work, k4 from LH needle, then k4 from cable needle.

Masterclass

How to knit a cable braid
Worked over 12 stitches, the right 8 stitches are twisted to the right (C8B) while the left 4 stitches are knitted plain then the right 4 stitches are knitted plain while the left 8 stitches are twisted to the left (C8F). The result is a staggered combination of the two eight-stitch cables, which results in a wonderful braid effect.

It is possible to make cables travel all over a piece of knitting by taking the cable stiches in any direction you wish. Just keep crossing over the stitches and making them travel across the knitting.

Why not work this pattern using any of the other cable stitches given in the Stitch Library (see pages 58–59).

To make the Cable Hot-water Bottle Cover
Front
Using 6 US (4mm) needles, cast on 48 sts and work 8 rows in k1, p1 rib as foll:
Rib row 1 (RS) [K1, p1] to end.
Rib row 2 [K1, p1] to end.
Rep last 2 rows 3 times more, ending with RS facing for next row.
Change to 7 US (4.5mm) needles and work in cable braid patt as foll:
Row 1 (RS) P3, [k12, p3] to end of row.
Row 2 K3, [p12, k3] to end of row.
Row 3 P3, [C8F, k4, p3] to end of row.
Row 4 K3, [p12, k3] to end of row.
Row 5 P3, [k12, p3] to end of row.
Row 6 K3, [p12, k3] to end of row.
Row 7 P3, [k12, p3] to end of row.
Row 8 K3, [p12, k3] to end of row.
Row 9 P4, [k4, C8B, p3] to end of row.
Row 10 K3, [p12, k3] to end of row.
Row 11 P3, [k12, p3] to end of row.
Row 12 K3, [p12, k3] to end of row.
Rep 12-row cable braid pattern 7 times in total.
84 rows worked; measures 14¼in/36cm from cast-on edge.

Shape top
Keeping patt correct, bind off 4 sts at beg of next 4 rows, then bind off 3 sts at beg of next 2 rows. *26 sts.*
Change to 6 US (4mm) needles and work 5½in/ 14cm in k1, p1 rib.
Bind off in rib.

Back
Work as given for Front but rep 12-row cable patt 3 times in total.
36 rows worked; measures 6¼in/16cm from cast-on edge.
Shape top as given for Front.

To finish
Weave in any loose yarn ends. *See Masterclass, page 67.*
Lay the work out flat and gently steam the finished piece on the reverse, taking care not to flatten the cables.
Pin the right sides of the Back and Front together, matching from the top.
Fold the front 5in/13cm from the cast-on edge toward the back so it overlaps onto the back.
Pin through all layers.
Using mattress stitch (see page 41) join the first 2¾in/7cm of the ribbing, then continue in backstitch and sew all around the cover, ensuring that you sew through all three layers where they overlap. Use mattress stitch for the last 2¾in/7cm of the ribbing. (This reverses the seam for the turtleneck of the cover.)
Turn cover right-side out and slip the hot-water bottle inside.

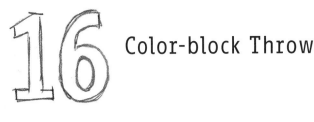

Color-block Throw

Here is my simple take on the basic "squares" blanket, a favorite project for beginner knitters. This patchwork throw is worked in one piece, so it requires no finishing other than weaving in a few yarn ends. The project introduces the technique called color blocking, or intarsia, where a new thread of yarn is used for each color change. Knitted in stockinette stitch, this graphic throw is made in an aran-weight cotton to give good stitch clarity as well as year-round comfort.

Skill level...

INTERMEDIATE

In this project you will learn...

Changing colors neatly using the color-block or intarsia method

Stitches used...

Stockinette stitch

Size

Finished size of throw: approximately 47½in/120cm wide by 57in/144cm long
Actual size of each color block: 9½in/24cm square

Materials

Medium-weight cotton yarn, such as Debbie Bliss Eco Fairtrade Cotton (4) MEDIUM
  A 11 x 1¾oz/50g balls (98yd/90m per ball) in black
  B 11 x 1¾oz/50g balls (98yd/90m per ball) in beige
Size 7 (4.5mm) circular knitting needle, 39in/100cm long

Gauge

18 stitches and 24 rows to 4in/10cm square over St st using 7 US (4.5mm) needles

Notes

Use a separate ball for each color and twist the yarns on the wrong side of the fabric when changing color to avoid a hole. *See Masterclass, on page 124.*
Where possible, weave in any loose yarn ends as you work. *See Masterclass, page 67.*

Masterclass

Changing yarn using the color-block (intarsia) method

When knitting using several colors across a row, organize the yarns into "bobbins"—small windings of individual yarns. To work out how much yarn you will need, calculate the number of stitches in that specific area then twist the yarn around the knitting needle that number of times, adding a small amount more for sewing in the ends. Once you have measured out the correct amount of yarn, either wind it into a small bobbin by hand or wrap it around a store-bought bobbin.

1 To join in a new color on a knit row, work up to the color change. Drop the old color. Pick up the new color from under the old color and knit to the next color change.
2 On a purl row, work up to the color change. Drop the old color. Pick up the new color from under the old color and purl to the next color change.

In effect, you are "twisting" the two colors around each other to link them together. Be careful not to overtwist the yarn or the fabric will not lie flat. The object is to link together the two separate color sections so that they form a single fabric.

To make the Color-block Throw

Cast on 210 sts in the following color sequence: 42A, 42B, 42A, 42B, 42A.
* First row of squares
Row 1 K42A, k42B, k42A, k42B, k42A.
Row 2 P42A, p42B, p42A, p42B, p42A.
These two rows set the squares for the first section of the throw.
Work 54 rows more as set.
Cut off yarn for each square, leaving yarn ends each about 6in/15cm long.
Second row of squares
Row 1 K42B, k42A, k42B, k42A, k42B.
Row 2 P42B, p42A, p42B, p42A, p42B.
These two rows set the squares for the second section of the throw.
Work 54 rows more as set.
Cut off yarn for each square, leaving yarn ends each about 6in/15cm long.
Rep from * twice more.
Six rows of squares have been worked.
Bind off, twisting yarns as the colors change.

To finish

Weave in any loose yarn ends. *See Masterclass, page 67.*
Lay the work out flat and gently steam the finished piece on the reverse.

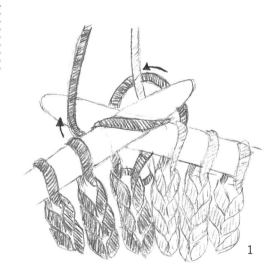

1

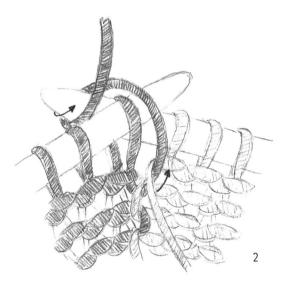

2

17 Fair Isle Pincushion

A small starter project to experiment with the "stranding" or Fair Isle technique, which involves knitting with two different color yarns across a row while following a simple stitch chart. Worked in contrasting black and white as a parody of the traditional Victorian-style lace patterns, this pincushion is perfect for keeping your sewing materials in order.

Skill level...

EXPERIENCED

In this project you will learn...

Working with two colors in one row using Fair Isle technique; making a picot edging

Stitches used...

Stockinette stitch

Size
Finished size of pincushion: approximately 4¾in/12cm by 2½in/6cm
Actual size of knitted pieces: approximately 4¾in/12cm by 2½in/6cm

Materials
2 x 9oz/245g cone (930yd/850m per cone) Super-fine-weight mercerized cotton yarn, such as Yeomans Cotton Cannele 4-Ply **①** SUPER FINE
1oz/25g of each of the following:
  A black
  B off-white
Pair of size 2 US (2.75mm) knitting needles
Small amount of stuffing

Gauge
32 stitches and 42 rows to 4in/10cm square over St st using 2 US (2.75mm) needles

To make the Pincushion
Front
Using yarn A, cast on 41 sts and beg with a knit row, work 10 rows in St st.
Work the 11 rows from the Fair Isle chart below, repeating the center 12 sts 3 times and ending with WS facing for next row. Cut off yarn B.
Using yarn A and beg with a purl row, work 10 rows in St st, ending with WS facing for next row. Bind off purlwise.

Back
Using yarn A, cast on 41 sts and beg with a knit row, work 31 rows in St st, ending with WS facing for next row. Bind off purlwise.

Simple picot edging
Using yarn A, cast on 5 sts. * Bind off 4 sts, slip rem st on RH needle onto LH needle, cast on 4 sts, rep from * until edging measures 16½in/42cm. Bind off.

To finish
Weave in any loose yarn ends. *See Masterclass, page 67.*
Lay the work out flat and gently steam the finished piece on the reverse.
Sew together three sides, leaving one side open for stuffing. Stuff firmly and close seam.
Sew edging to pincushion along seamline.

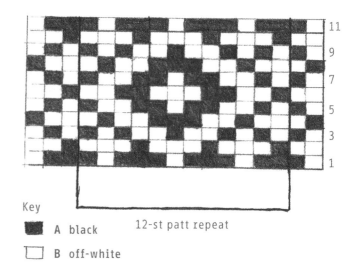

Key

■ A black   12-st patt repeat

□ B off-white

Masterclass

Fair Isle technique (stranding)

When knitting with two or three colors in a row, you can strand the color not in use loosely across the back of the knitted fabric until it is needed again. This colorwork technique is called Fair Isle. I have consciously designed this pincushion as a simple Fair Isle, ensuring that each of the two colors in the row is used over no more than three stitches. (When a color is used over more than three stitches in a multicolor row it has to be woven into the back of the work.)

1 On a knit row, drop the working yarn. Bring the new color over the top of the dropped yarn and work to the next color change.
2 Drop the working yarn. Bring the new color under the dropped yarn and work to the next color change. Repeat these two steps for all subsequent color changes in the row.

1 On a purl row, drop the working yarn. Bring the new color over the top of the dropped yarn and work to the next color change.
2 Drop the working yarn. Bring the new color under the dropped yarn and work to the next color change. Repeat these two steps for all subsequent color changes in the row.

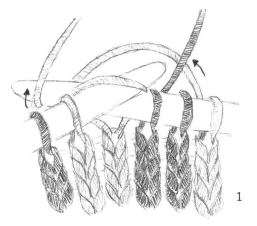

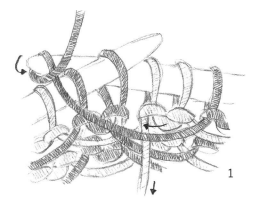

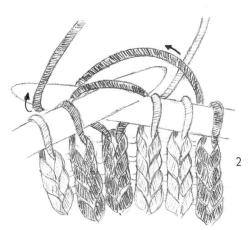

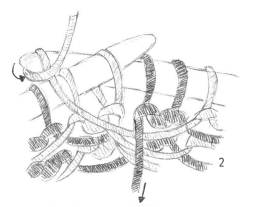

Rose Teapot Cozy

A basic teapot cozy knitted in stockinette stitch decorated with a pretty rose design worked in muted vintage colors. For ease, the base colors of the rose motifs are knitted using the intarsia method, while the extra highlights and shading are embroidered over the top with duplicate stitch. Apart from the two main colors, only small amounts of the other shades are needed, so this is the perfect project for using up scrap or stash yarns.

Skill level...

EXPERIENCED

In this project you will learn...

Adding color using duplicate stitch

Stitches used...

Stockinette stitch

Size
Finished size of teapot cozy: to fit average size teapot

Materials
Double-knitting-weight wool yarn, such as Rowan Cashsoft DK or Rowan Pure Wool DK **(3)** LIGHT
or
4-Ply wool yarn used double, such as Rowan Cashsoft 4-Ply **(1)** SUPER FINE
    A 2 x 1¾oz/50g balls (142yd/130m per ball) in stone
    B 1 x 1¾oz/50g ball (142yd/130m per ball) in pink
    C small amount (6yd/5m) in purple
    D small amount (8yd/7m) in teal
    E small amount (6yd/5m) in gold
    F small amount (8yd/7m) ball in sage green
    G small amount (6yd/5m) in brown
    H small amount (11yd/10m) in amethyst
    I small amount (8yd/7m) ball in ecru
    J small amount (6yd/5m) in dark gray
    K small amount (13yd/12m) in taupe
Pair each of sizes 3 US (3.25mm) and 6 US (4mm) knitting needles
Fabric and batting, for lining
4in/10cm of narrow woven cotton tape

Gauge
22 stitches and 30 rows to 4in/10cm square over St st using 6 US (4mm) needles

Note
Work decreases 2 sts in from the edge as foll:
On a knit row: k2, k2tog, k to last 4 sts, k2tog tbl, k2.
On a purl row: p2, p2tog tbl, p to last 4 sts, p2tog, p2.

To make the Rose Teapot Cozy
Front
Using 3 US (3.25mm) needles and yarn B, cast on 70 sts and work 4 rows in k1, pl 1 rib.
Change to yarn A and work 1 row rib.
Change to yarn B and work 4 rows rib.
Change to 6 US (4mm) needles and yarn A, and beg with a purl row, work 36 rows in St st without shaping, ending with WS facing for next row and AT SAME TIME work chart rows 10–45 on page 131 using the intarsia technique (page 124) to work the outlined flower shapes in yarns K and B and the background in yarn A (the other details on top of the flowers and around the flowers are worked later in duplicate stitch).
Cont to work motifs following chart, shape top of cozy as foll:
Dec 1 st at each end of next row. *68 sts.*
Work 3 rows without shaping.
Dec 1 st at each end of next row. *66 sts.*
Work 2 rows without shaping.

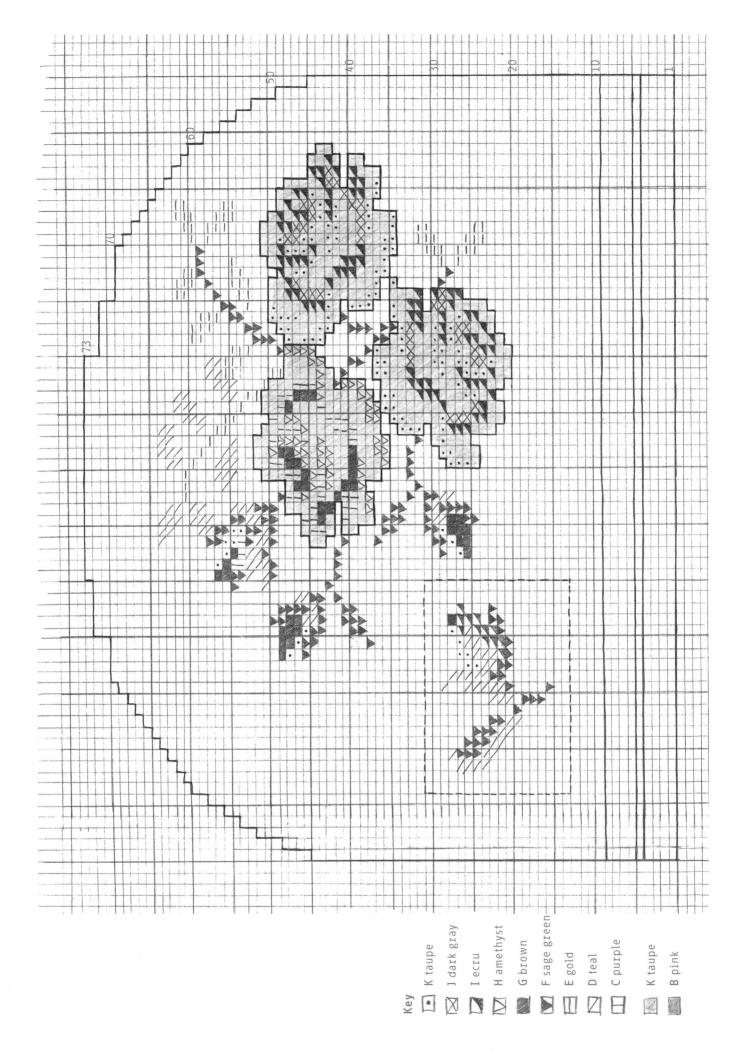

Key

- K taupe
- J dark gray
- I ecru
- H amethyst
- G brown
- F sage green
- E gold
- D teal
- C purple
- K taupe
- B pink

Next row Dec 1 st at each end of next and every alt row until 58 sts remain.
Work 1 row.
Dec 1 st at each end of next 9 rows. *40 sts*
Bind off 5 sts at beg of next 4 rows. *20 sts*
Work 1 row.
Bind off.

Back
Work as for Front, but use yarn A only for St st section.

To finish
Following the chart, embroider the details on the Front in duplicate stitch (see right), omitting the small bud motif in lower left of chart—work this motif on the Back only.
Weave in any loose yarn ends. *See Masterclass, page 67.*
Lay the work out flat and gently steam the finished piece on the reverse.
With right sides together, sew seam all around curved edge, leaving a 1.5cm opening at top. Turn right-side out.
Fold tape in half, insert into opening and sew into position to make the hanging loop.
Cut two pieces of batting the same size and shape as the cover. Repeat for lining but add 1.5cm seam allowance all around.
Sew batting pieces together, stitching close to the edge. Do not turn inside out.
With right sides of lining pieces together, sew around curved edge 1/2in/1.5cm from edge.
Without turning right-side out, insert lining inside batting "pocket."
Insert into knitted cozy, turn up lower edge of lining and sew to cozy all around hem.

Masterclass

Duplicate stitch
Duplicate stitch is a form of embroidery made to look like knit stitches. Using a blunt-ended yarn needle and yarn, you can sew small areas of color over the top of knitted stitches to add decorative detail without having to use the tricky technique of knitting with multiple colors. To knit each of the colored stitches that make up the rose motif on this teapot cozy would be incredibly difficult and challenge even the most proficient knitter. I think you will get a far better result by embroidering the odd highlight color over a base color. But do make sure when you are working duplicate stitch over the top of the knitted stitches, not to pull the embroidered stitches too tight as this will pucker the fabric.

1 To work a horizontal row of duplicate stitch, work from right to left across the knitted fabric. Bring the needle through from the back of the fabric at the base of a stitch, then take it under the two loops at the base of the stitch above.
2 Insert the needle back through to the back of the fabric where it first came out at the base of the lower stitch and take it across to come out at the base of the next stitch to the left. One duplicate stitch is complete.

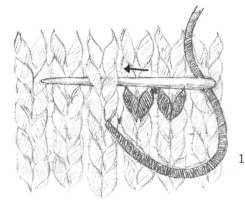
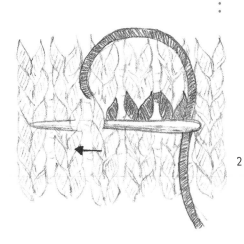

Woman's V-neck Sweater

A simple sweater knitted in basic stockinette stitch with rib edgings. This design will work in most double-knitting-weight yarns. Here it is made in a soft pima cotton, but it would be equally beautiful in merino, linen, or alpaca. The design is classic V-neck with defined fully fashioned detailing made by paired increases and decreases. A truly perennial piece.

Skill level...

EXPERIENCED

In this project you will learn...

Fully fashioned shaping; picking up stitches

Stitches used...

Stockinette stitch; k1, p1 rib

Size

To fit bust	XS	S	M	L	XL	
	32	34	36	38	40	in
	81	86	91	97	102	cm
Actual bust	33¹⁄₂	36	37³⁄₄	40¹⁄₄	41¹⁄₂	in
	85.5	91	96	102	105.5	cm
Length	22	23	23¹⁄₂	24¹⁄₂	25	in
to back neck	56	58	60	62	64	cm
Sleeve	16¹⁄₂	17¹⁄₂	18	18	19	in
	42	44	46	46	48	cm

Materials

8 (9: 10: 11: 12) x 1¾oz/50g balls (142yd/120m per ball) of double-knitting-weight yarn, such as Rowan Pima Cotton DK ⓷ LIGHT

Pair each of sizes 3 US (3.25mm) and 6 US (4mm) knitting needles

Gauge

22 stitches and 30 rows to 4in/10cm square over St st using 6 US (4mm) needles

Note

Work all the increases and decreases three stitches in from the edges to create fully fashioned shaping. *See Masterclass, page 107.*

To make the Woman's V-neck Sweater
Back

Using 3 US (3.25mm) needles, cast on 97 (103: 109: 115: 119) sts and work in k1, p1 rib as foll:
Row 1 (RS) K1, * p1, k1, rep from * to end.
Row 2 * P1, k1, rep from * to last st, p1.
These 2 rows set k1, p1 rib.
Cont in k1, p1 rib as set until work measures 2in/5cm and AT THE SAME TIME dec 1 st at end of last row. *96 (102: 108: 114: 118) sts.*
Change to 6 US (4mm) needles and beg with a k row, work in St st until work measures 14¹⁄₂ (15: 15¹⁄₄: 15³⁄₄: 16)in/37 (38: 39: 40: 41)cm, ending with RS facing for next row.
Shape armholes
Bind off 5 sts at beg of next 2 rows.
86 (92: 98: 104: 108) sts.
Working dec as above (see Note), dec 1 st at each end of next 5 rows.
76 (82: 88: 94: 98) sts
Working dec as set throughout, dec 1 st at each end of next row and 2 foll alt rows.
70 (76: 82: 88: 92) sts
Cont without shaping until armhole measures 7 (7¹⁄₂: 7³⁄₄: 8¹⁄₄: 8¹⁄₂)in/18 (19: 20: 21: 22)cm, ending with RS facing for next row.
Shape shoulders and back neck
Bind off 5 (5: 6: 7: 7) sts at beg of next 2 rows.
60 (66: 70: 74: 78) sts.
Next row Bind off 5 (6: 6: 7: 7) sts, knit until there are 9 (10: 11: 11: 11) sts on RH needle, then turn, leaving rem sts on a stitch holder.
Cont on these 9 (10: 11: 11: 11) sts only as foll:
Next row (WS) Bind off 4 sts, purl to end.
Bind off rem 5 (6: 7: 7: 7) sts.
Return to rem sts and with RS facing, slip center 32 (34: 36: 38: 42) sts on a st holder, then rejoin

yarn to rem 14 (16: 17: 18: 18) sts and knit to end.
Complete to match first side, reversing all
shaping.

Front
Work as given for Back to start of armhole
shaping, ending with RS facing for next row.
Shape armholes
Bind off 5 sts at beg of next 2 rows.
86 (92: 98: 104: 108) sts.
Working dec as set on Back throughout, dec 1 st
at each end of next 2 rows.
82 (88: 94: 100: 104) sts.
Divide and shape neck
Working all dec as set, cont as foll:
Next row (RS) K3, k2tog, knit until there are
35 (38: 41: 43: 46) sts on RH needle, k2tog tbl, k3,
then turn, leaving rem sts on a st holder.
Cont on these 39 (42: 45: 48: 50) sts only as foll:
Work 4 rows, dec 1 st at neck edge on 2nd and 4th
rows, and AT THE SAME TIME dec 1 st at armhole
edge in every row.
33 (36: 39: 42: 44) sts.
Work 3 rows, dec 1 st at each end of 2nd row.
31 (34: 37: 40: 42) sts.
Dec 1 st at neck edge only on next row and every
foll alt row until there are 16 (20: 22: 25: 24) sts
then on every foll 4th row until there are 15 (17:
19: 21: 21) sts.
Cont without shaping until armhole matches Back
to start of shoulder shaping, ending with RS
facing for next row.
Shape shoulder
Bind off 5 (5: 6: 7: 7) sts at beg of next row.
Work 1 row.
Bind off 5 (6: 6: 7: 7) sts at beg of next row.
Work 1 row.
Bind off rem 5 (6: 7: 7: 7) sts.
With RS facing, rejoin yarn to rem sts, k3, k2tog,
knit to last 5 sts, k2tog tbl, k3.
39 (42: 45: 48: 50) sts.
Complete to match first side, reversing all
shaping.

Sleeves (make 2)
Using 3 US (3.25mm) needles, cast on 59 (61: 63: 65:
65) sts.
Work in k1, p1 rib as given for Back until work
measures 2¾in/7cm, ending with RS facing for
next row.
Change to 6 US (4mm) needles and beg with a k
row, cont in St st and AT THE SAME TIME working

incs as explained in Note on page 134, inc 1 st at
each end of 11th row and every foll 20th (16th:
14th: 12th: 10th) row until there are 69 (73: 77:
81: 85) sts.
Cont without shaping until sleeve measures
16½ (17½: 18: 18: 19)in/42 (44: 46: 46: 48)cm,
ending with RS facing for next row.
Shape top of sleeve
Bind off 5 sts at beg of next 2 rows.
59 (63: 67: 71: 75) sts.
Working dec as set on Front and Back, dec 1 st
at each end of next 5 rows, then on every foll alt
row until 23 sts rem.
Dec 1 st at each end of next 5 rows.
Bind off rem 13 sts.

To finish
Lay the finished pieces out flat and gently steam
on the reverse.
Sew right shoulder seam.
Neckband
With RS facing and using 3 US (3.25mm) needles,
pick up and knit 43 (45: 47: 49: 51) sts down left
side of neck, place marker on needle, pick up
and knit 43 (45: 47: 49: 51) sts up right side of
neck and 4 sts down right side of back neck, knit
across 32 (34: 36: 38: 42) sts from holder at back
neck, and pick up and knit 3 sts up left side of
back neck.
125 (131: 137: 143: 151) sts.
Work in k1, p1, rib as foll:
Row 1 (WS) Beg with a k1, work in k1, p1 rib over
first 43 (45: 47: 49: 51) sts (ending with k1), slip
marker onto RH needle, beg with k1, work in k1,
p1 rib to end.
Row 2 Rib as set to 2 sts before marker, k2tog
tbl, slip marker onto RH needle, k2tog, rib to end.
Row 3 Rib as set to 2 sts before marker, p2tog,
slip marker onto RH needle, p2tog tbl, rib to end.
Rep last 2 rows until neckband measures
1in/2.5cm.
Bind off in rib.
Sew left shoulder and neckband seam. Set in
sleeves. Sew side and sleeve seams.
Weave in any loose yarn ends. *See Masterclass,
page 67.*
For optional cotton tape inside back neckband,
see page 81.

Masterclass

Picking up stitches along a neck edge

Adding a well-knitted neckband can really make a garment. It is possible to knit a neckband separately and then sew it in place but I prefer to pick up stitches around the neck edge and knit on the neckband.

To ensure that your neckband is knitted evenly all around the neck edge, before you start picking up stitches divide the area into even sections and mark each with a pin or contrasting color yarn. Divide the number of stitches to be picked up by the number of sections marked out and that is the number of stitches to be picked up in each section. For example, if you need to pick up 48 stitches and you have divided your neck edge up into 8 sections, then you need to pick up 6 stitches in each section. I find it far easier to pick up 6 stitches evenly over a small area than it is to judge 48 stitches over an entire neck edge.

To pick up a stitch, from the front of the fabric put the tip of the knitting needle into the space between the edge stitch and the next stitch. Wrap the working yarn around the needle. Bring the needle and the working yarn through to the front of the work. Continue in this way until the required numbers of stitches have been picked up.

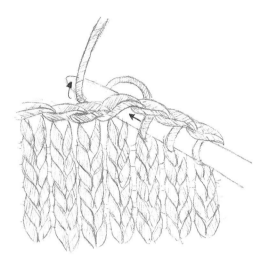

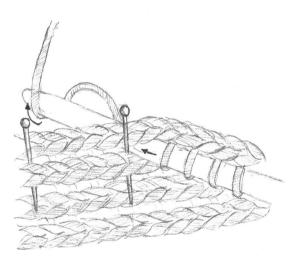

Woman's Pocket Cardigan

A timeless cardigan knitted in luxuriously soft baby alpaca yarn with a deep V-neck, integral button bands, pockets, and fully fashioned shaping (see page 107). Fastened with large mother of-pearl buttons, this a truly classic garment.

Skill level...

██ ██ ██ ▬▬
EXPERIENCED

In this project you will learn...

Knitting in pockets

Stitches used...

Stockinette stitch; k1, p1 rib

Size

To fit bust	XS	S	M	L	XL	
	32	34	36	38	40	in
	81	86	91	97	102	cm
Actual bust	33¾	36¼	38¼	40½	41¾	in
	86	92	97	102.5	106	cm
Length to back neck	25½	26½	27¼	28	28¾	in
	65	67	69	71	73	cm
Sleeve	16½	17½	18	18	19	in
	42	44	46	46	48	cm

Materials

12 (13: 13: 14: 15) x 1¾oz/50g balls (109yd/100m per ball) double-knitting-weight wool yarn, such as Rowan Baby Alpaca DK **(3)** LIGHT
Pair each of sizes 3 US (3.25mm) and 6 US (4mm) knitting needles
5 buttons, ⁷⁄₈in/22mm in diameter

Gauge

22 stitches and 30 rows to 4in/10cm square over St st using 6 US (4mm) needles

To make the Woman's Pocket Cardigan
Back
Using 3 US (3.25mm) needles, cast on 97 (103: 109: 115: 119) sts.
Row 1 (RS) K1, * p1, k1, rep from * to end.
Row 2 * P1, k1, rep from * to last st, p1.
These 2 rows set k1, p1 rib.
Work 14 rows more in rib as set, ending with RS facing for next row.
Change to 6 US (4mm) needles and beg with a k row, work in St st until work measures 18 (18½: 18¾: 19¼: 19¾)in/46 (47: 48: 49: 50)cm, ending with RS facing for next row.
Shape armholes
Bind off 5 sts at beg of next 2 rows. *87 (93: 99: 105: 109) sts.*
Working fully fashioned decreases as for V-neck (see Note, page 134), dec 1 st at each end of next 5 rows. *77 (83: 89: 95: 99) sts.*
Working dec as set throughout, dec 1 st at each end of next and 2 foll alt rows. *71 (77: 83: 89: 93) sts.*
Cont without shaping until armhole measures 7 (7½: 7¾: 8¼: 8½)in/18 (19: 20: 21: 22)cm, ending with RS facing for next row.
Shape shoulders and back neck
Bind off 5 (6: 7: 8: 8) sts at beg of next 2 rows. *61 (65: 69: 73: 77) sts.*
Next row Bind off 5 (6: 7: 8: 8) sts, knit until there are 10 (11: 11: 12: 13) sts on the needle, then turn, leaving rem sts on a stitch holder.
Cont on these 10 (11: 11: 12: 13) sts only as foll:
Bind off 4 sts at beg of next row. *6 (7: 7: 8: 9) sts.*
Bind off rem 6 (7: 7: 8: 9) sts.
With RS facing, rejoin yarn to rem sts, bind off center 31 (31: 33: 33: 35) sts, and knit to end.
Bind off 5 (6: 7: 8: 8) sts at beg of next row. *10 (11: 11: 12: 13) sts.*
Bind off 4 sts at beg of next row.
Bind off rem 6 (7: 7: 8: 9) sts.

Pocket linings (make 2)
Using 6 US (4mm) needles, cast on 29 sts and beg with a knit row, work 5½in/14cm in St st, ending with RS facing for next row.
Dec 1 st at each end of next row. *27 sts.*
Leave stitches on a holder.

Left front
Using 3 US (3.25mm) needles, cast on 53 (57: 59: 63: 65) sts.
Work 16 rows in rib as set on Back, ending with RS facing for next row.

Change to 6 US (4mm) needles and work as foll:
Row 1 (RS) Knit to last 12 sts, rib as set to end.
Row 2 Rib first 12 sts as set, purl to end.
Rep these 2 rows until work measures 6¼in/16cm from cast-on edge, ending with RS facing for next row.
Work pocket top as foll:
Next row K6 (10: 12: 16: 18); [k1, p1] 13 times, k1 (pocket top); k to last 12 sts, rib 12 as set.
Next row Rib 12, p8; rib 27 as set (pocket top); p6 (10: 12: 16: 18).
Rep last 2 rows 3 times more.
Next row K6 (10: 12: 16: 18), bind off next 27 sts in rib, work to end as set.
Next row Rib 12, p8, with WS of pocket facing p 27 sts from one holder, work to end as set. *53 (57: 59: 63: 65) sts.*
Pocket lining is now part of the cardigan front.
Work even with rib edging as set until work measures 14¼ (14½: 15: 15½: 15¾)in/36 (37: 38: 39: 40)cm from cast-on edge, ending with RS facing for next row.
Shape front slope
Next row (dec row) Work to last 17 sts, k2tog tbl, k3, rib 12.
Next row Rib 12, work to end of row.
Working dec as set on Back throughout, dec 1 st at neck edge on 3rd row and 4 foll 6th rows. *47 (51: 53: 57: 59) sts.*
Work 1 row, ending with RS facing for next row.
Front now matches Back to start of armhole shaping.
Shape armhole
Next row Bind off 5 sts, knit to end. *42 (46: 48: 52: 54) sts.*
Next row Purl.
Working dec as set, dec 1 st at armhole edge on next 5 rows, then on 3 foll alt rows and AT SAME TIME dec 1 st at neck edge on 3rd row and foll 6th row. *32 (36: 38: 42: 44) sts.*
Keeping armhole straight, cont to dec at front edge on 4th row and every foll 6th row until 30 (33: 36: 36: 37) sts remain.
For 1st, 2nd, and 3rd sizes only
Dec 1 st at neck edge on every foll 8th row until there are 28 (31: 33) sts.
For all 5 sizes
Cont without shaping until armhole matches Back to start of shoulder shaping, ending with RS facing for next row.
Next row Bind off 5 (6: 7: 8: 8) sts and work to last 12 sts, then turn, leaving the 12 rib sts on a st holder. *11 (13: 14: 16: 17) sts.*

Work 1 row.
Bind off 5 (6: 7: 8: 8) sts at beg of next row.
Work 1 row. Bind off rem 6 (7: 7: 8: 9) sts.

Right front
Using 3 US (3.25mm) needles, cast on 53 (57: 59: 63: 65) sts.
Work 8 rows in rib as set on Back.
Buttonhole row 1 (RS) Rib 5 sts, bind off next 2 sts, rib to end.
Buttonhole row 2 Rib as set, casting on 2 sts over those bound off in previous row.
Work 6 rows more in rib, ending with RS facing for next row.
Change to 6 US (4mm) needles and working 4 more buttonholes at 3¼in/8.5cm intervals, cont as foll:
Row 1 (RS) Rib 12 sts as set, knit to end.
Row 2 Purl to last 12 sts, rib as set.
Rep last 2 rows until work measures 6¼in/16cm from cast-on edge, ending with RS facing for next row. *Don't forget to work the buttonholes.*
Work pocket top as foll:
Next row Rib 12, k8; (k1, p1) 13 times, k1; k to end.
Next row P6 (10: 12: 16: 18); rib 27 as set; p8, rib 12.
Repeat last 2 rows three times more.
Next row Rib 12, k8, bind off next 27 sts in rib, work to end as set.
Next row P6 (10: 12: 16: 18), then with WS of pocket lining facing, p 27 sts from st holder, purl to last 12 sts, rib as set. *53 (57: 59: 63: 65) sts.*
Pocket lining is now part of the cardigan front.
Work even as set until work measures 14¼ (14½: 15: 15½: 15¾)in/36 (37: 38: 39: 40)cm from cast-on edge, ending RS facing for next row.
Shape front slope
Next row (dec row) Rib 12, k3, k2tog, knit to end.
Next row Purl to last 12 sts, rib 12.
Working dec as set on Back throughout, dec 1 st at neck edge on 3rd row and 4 foll 6th rows. *47 (51: 53: 57: 59) sts.*
Work 2 rows, ending with WS facing for next row.
Front now matches Back to start of armhole shaping.
Shape armhole
Bind off 5 sts at beg of next row. *42 (46: 48: 52: 54) sts.*
Working dec as set, dec 1 st at neck edge on 3rd row and foll 6th row and AT SAME TIME dec 1 st at armhole edge on next 5 rows, then on 3 foll alt rows. *32 (36: 38: 42: 44) sts.*
Keeping armhole straight, cont to dec at front edge on 4th row and every foll 6th row until 30 (33: 36: 36: 37) sts remain.

For 1st, 2nd, and 3rd sizes only
Dec 1 st at neck edge on every foll 8th row until
there are 28 (31: 33) sts.
For all sizes
Cont without shaping until armhole matches Back
to start of shoulder shaping, ending with WS
facing for next row.
Next row Bind off 5 (6: 7: 8: 8) sts and work to
last 12 sts, then turn, leaving 12 rib sts on a st
holder. *11 (13: 14: 16: 17) sts.*
Work 1 row.
Bind off 5 (6: 7: 8: 8) sts at beg of next row.
Work 1 row. Bind off rem 6 (7: 7: 8: 9) sts.

Sleeves (make 2)

Using 3 US (3.25mm) needles, cast on 59 (61: 63: 65:
65) sts.
Work in k1, p1 rib as for Back until work measures
2¾in/7cm, ending with RS facing for next row.
Change to 6 US (4mm) needles and beg with a k
row, cont in St st and AT SAME TIME working incs
as explained in Note on pge 134, inc 1 st at each
end of 11th and every foll 20th (16th: 14th: 12th:
10th) row until there are 69 (73: 77: 81: 85) sts.
Cont without shaping until sleeve measures
16½ (17½: 18: 18: 19)in/42 (44: 46: 46: 48)cm,
ending with RS facing for next row.
Shape top of sleeve
Bind off 5 sts at beg of next 2 rows. *59 (63: 67:
71: 75) sts.*
Working dec as set on Back, dec 1 st at each end
of next 5 rows, then on every foll alt row until
23 sts rem.
Dec 1 st at each end of next 5 rows.
Bind off rem 13 sts.

To finish

Weave in any loose yarn ends.
Gently steam pieces on the reverse.
Sew both shoulder seams.
Back neckband
Using 6 US (4mm) needles, rejoin yarn to 12 sts of
right front band and cont in rib as set until band
when slightly stretched, reaches center back.
Leave stitches on holder.
Repeat for left front band, then graft two sets of
stitches together and sew neckband in place.
Sew pocket linings to inside (see right).
Set in sleeves. Sew side and sleeve seams.
Sew on buttons to match buttonholes.
For optional cotton tape inside back neckband,
see page 81.

Masterclass

Pockets

A classic cardigan should always have pockets.
There are several ways of making pockets, but
my preferred method is to knit them integrally
to ensure pockets are level, neat, and require
very little sewing up at the end of the project.

First, knit the pocket lining by casting on
the number of stitches needed to achieve the
required width. Work to the depth of pocket
required and leave these stitches on a holder.

On the row where you want the pocket, work
the stitches for the pocket top in k1, p1 rib
while keeping the stitches on either side in
pattern. Once the pocket tops are the correct
depth, bind off the pocket-top stitches in rib.

On the next row work the pocket lining
stitches from the holder in place of the bound-
off pocket-top rib stitches. Then continue the
rest of the garment.

To keep pocket linings square when sewing
them in place, use a contrasting color
thread to baste guidelines between stitches
along each side of the pocket opening. Then
slipstitch the pocket linings down following
the basted guidelines.

Recommended yarns

There is a yarn specified for each of the twenty designs in the Project Workshops section of this book. If you can stick to the recommended yarn, you just need to pick your preferred shade. However, if you want to use a different yarn to the one specified, you need to compare the gauges given to ensure the finished result will not differ too wildly.

There are standard weights—or thicknesses—of yarns, recognized throughout the spinner's industry. Hand-knit yarns commonly range from fingering through sport, double knitting, and worsted to super bulky at the opposite end of the scale. Within each of these categories there is a degree of tolerance, so it is still important to check the gauge of each yarn against that given in a pattern (see Gauge, pages 36–37).

Each yarn will have slightly varying physical properties from the next and will perform differently. Some yarns may be colorfast and easycare while others may only be suitable for dry-cleaning or could possibly felt if not treated correctly (see Aftercare, page 47). The care information for a yarn will be given on the yarn label that comes wrapped around a ball, hank, or skein. I always keep a yarn label for each project that I make—and if I give a hand knit as a gift, I include the yarn label so the recipient knows how to care for the item. When you invest so much of your time and energy into creating a hand-knitted item, great care should be taken in the laundering.

Alongside the manufacturer's brand name and the name given to the specific yarn, a yarn label will typically carry the following information:

Average gauge and recommended knitting needle sizes
This is the spinner's recommended gauge and needle size. However, a designer may vary from this recommendation within a pattern; if so, always go with the designer's recommendation.

Weight of yarn
Provided in ounces or grams, most yarns come in either 1.75oz/50g or 3.5oz/100g balls.

Length of yarn in ball
The approximate length of yarn in the ball is just as important to consider as gauge when considering a substitute yarn.

Fiber composition
A yarn label will list the materials that the yarn is made from, whether that is 100% pure wool or a blend of fibers such as cotton and silk. This affects not just the method of care for the finished item, but also the suitability of a yarn for a certain project.

Shade and dye-lot numbers
Each shade of yarn is given an identifying name and/or number by the manufacturer. When purchasing yarn the dye-lot number is equally, if not more important, as this number needs to be the same on every ball. As yarn is dyed in batches, buying yarn with the same dye-lot numbers ensures there will be no color variations between balls.

Care instructions
A yarn label will indicate whether the yarn is suitable for machine washing or should be dry-cleaned only, and whether or not it can be ironed and, if so, at what temperature. This information is usually given in the form of standard international care symbols.

Alchemy Yarns Silken Straw: A fine-weight silk yarn; 100% silk; 236yd/215m per 40g; gauge—24 sts per 4in/10cm over St st using 4 US (3.5mm) needles.

Blue Sky Alpacas Royal: A fine-weight alpaca yarn; 100% alpaca; 288yd/263m per 100g; gauge—24–28 sts per 4in/10cm over St st using 2–3 US (2.75–3.25mm) needles.

Blue Sky Alpacas Worsted Hand Dyes: A medium-weight alpaca-blend yarn; 50% alpaca, 50% merino; 100yd/91m per 100g; gauge—16 sts per 4in/10cm over St st using 9 US (5.5mm) needles.

Debbie Bliss Como: A super-bulky-weight wool-blend yarn; 90% wool, 10% cashmere; 46yd/42m per 50g; gauge—10 sts x 15 rows per 4in/10cm over St st using 15 US (10mm) needles.

Debbie Bliss Eco Fairtrade Cotton: A medium-weight cotton yarn; 100% cotton; 99yd/90m per 50g; gauge—18 sts x 24 rows per 4in/10cm over St st using 7 US (4.5mm) needles.

Habu Cotton Gima: A super-fine-weight cotton yarn; 100% cotton; 258yd/236m per 28g; gauge—36 sts x 48 rows per 4in/10cm over St st using 2–3 US (2.25mm–3.25mm) needles.

Habu Silk Gima: A fine-weight silk yarn; 100% silk; 258yd/236m per 28g; gauge—26 sts x 36 rows per 4in/10cm over St st using 2–3 US (2.25mm–3.25mm) needles.

Jarol King Dishcloth Cotton: A medium-weight cotton yarn; 100% cotton; gauge—20 sts x 32 rows per 4in/10cm over St st using 7 US (4.5mm) needles.

Regia 4-Ply Erika Knight Design Line: A super-fine-weight wool-blend yarn; 75% wool, 25% polyamide; 229yd/115m per 50g; gauge—30 sts x 42 rows per 4in/10cm over St st using 2 US (2.75mm) needles.

Rowan Big Wool: A super-bulky-weight wool yarn; 100% merino; 87yd/80m per 50g; gauge—7.5 sts x 9 rows per 4in/10cm over St st using 15 US (10mm) or 19 US (15mm) needles.

Rowan British Sheeps Breed DK: A lightweight wool yarn; 100% wool; 131yd/120m per 50g ball; gauge—22 sts x 30 rows per 4in/10cm over St st using 6 US (4mm) needles.

Rowan Cashsoft Aran: A medium-weight merino blend yarn; 57% merino, 33% acrylic microfiber, 10% cashmere; 95yd/87m per 50g; gauge—19 sts x 25 rows per 4in/10cm over St st using 7 US (4.5mm) needles.

Rowan Cashsoft DK: A lightweight wool-blend yarn; 57% merino, 33% acrylic microfiber, 10% cashmere; 142yd/130m per 50g; gauge—22 sts x 30 rows per 4in/10cm over St st using 6 US (4mm) needles.

Rowan Cashsoft 4-Ply: A super-fine-weight wool-blend yarn; 57% merino, 33% acrylic microfiber, 10% cashmere; 197yd/180m per 50g; gauge—28 sts x 36 rows per 4in/10cm over St st using 3 US (3.25mm) needles.

Rowan Baby Alpaca DK: A lightweight alpaca yarn; 100% baby alpaca; 109yd/100m per 50g; gauge—22 sts x 30 rows per 4in/10cm over St st using 6 US (4mm) needles.

Rowan Kidsilk Aura: A medium-weight mohair-blend yarn; 75% kidsilk mohair, 25% silk; 82yd/75m per 25g; gauge—16–20 sts x 19–28 rows per 4in/10cm over St st using 6–10 US (4mm–6mm) needles.

Rowan Lenpur Linen: A lightweight linen-blend yarn; 75% VI Lenpur, 25% linen; 126yd/115m per 50g; gauge—22 sts x 30 rows per 4in/10cm over St st using 6 US (4mm) needles.

Rowan Pima Cotton DK: A lightweight cotton yarn; 100% pima cotton; 142yd/130m per 50g; gauge—22 sts x 30 rows per 4in/10cm over St st using 6 US (4mm) needles.

Rowan Pure Silk DK: A lightweight silk yarn; 100% silk; 137yd/125m per 50g; gauge—22 sts x 30 rows per 4in/10cm over St st using 6 US (4mm) needles.

Rowan Pure Wool DK: A lightweight wool yarn; 100% wool; 137yd/125m per 50g; gauge—22 sts x 30 rows per 4in/10cm over St st using 6 US (4mm) needles.

Yeoman's Cotton Cannele 4-Ply: A super-fine-weight cotton yarn; 100% mercerized cotton; 930yd/850m per 245g cone; gauge—33 sts x 44 rows per 4in/10cm over St st using 2 US (2.75mm) needles.

Knitting Needle Sizes

The systems of sizing needles are different in the US and UK. The standard US needle sizes and the closest UK metric sizes are as follows:

US	Metric	US	Metric
50	25mm	8	5mm
35	19mm	7	4.5mm
19	15mm	6	4mm
17	12mm	5	3.75mm
15	10mm	4	3.5mm
13	9mm	3	3.25mm
11	8mm	—	3mm
—	7.5mm	2	2.75mm
—	7mm	1	2.25mm
10½	6.5mm	0	2mm
10	6mm	00	1.75mm
9	5.5mm	000	1.5mm

Acknowledgments

In spite of its simple title and ethos, this has been a complex book to put together. It has involved the very best people of the highest caliber with the most discerning eyes, exacting standards, meticulous attention to detail, and above all unbelievable patience, for which I am enormously grateful and I would like to extend my heartfelt appreciation for their huge contributions. It is a privilege to work with them and certainly this book would not have happened without them.

The truly wonderful team at Quadrille. To my Editorial Director, and indeed mentor, Jane O'Shea. To my project editor Lisa Pendreigh—my sincerest thanks for her professionalism, exceptional expertise, patience, and personal support—as well as designer Claire Peters for her emphatic and creative design. And Ruth Deary for doing such a fabulous job in the production of the book.

It has been fabulous to have Yuki Sugiura photograph this book; her ease, empathy, and natural sense of style is central to the sensibility of this book. And, of course, Lara for assisting and for all things culinary and cool. My thanks, too, to our stylist Charis, for her diligence in the detail; she always had it there.

To my brilliant project maker, problem solver, and personal friend Sally Lee, enormously grateful for her misspent, or rather well-spent, youth crafting, knitting, sewing, and making stuff, all of which has paid off. To Sarah Hatton for gracing this book with her expertise and presence and Eileen Bundie for knitting par excellence. And, of course, technically Gina Alton, for her inestimable and meticulous work in pattern checking. Thanks, too, to Ian Harris for his wise, succinct, and supportive critique.

As people who know me will testify, I pore over all the detail all the time, but the selection of yarn is paramount to me and most especially when designing and offering projects of simple design. Hence my sincerest thanks and appreciation to the following creators of exceptional yarns of rare distinction for their generosity and enthusiastic support: as always the iconic yarn brand of Rowan, Regia, Habu, Gina Wilde of Alchemy, Blue Sky Alpacas, Debbie Bliss Designer Yarns, and Yeoman's Yarns, for constantly producing desirable fibers and yarns of excellent quality which entice and excite the creative soul. Long may you continue to do so.

Finally this book is dedicated to creatives and crafters everywhere, especially to the new breed of artisan entrepreneurs who are emerging and growing in number and confidence: who continually excite with their passion for the hand made, who constantly push the boundaries of craft with their enthusiasm, innovation, and origination. The future is yours!

Publisher's Acknowledgments
The publisher would like to thank the following for loaning accessories and other items:

THE ISLE MILL
Macnaughton Holdings Ltd, Tower House, Ruthvenfield Road, Perth PH1 3UN, UK
Tel: +44 1738-609090

ERCOL
Summerleys Road, Princes Risborough, Buckinghamshire HP27 9PX, UK
Tel: +44 1844-271800

FANNY'S ANTIQUES
1 Lynmouth Road, Reading, Berkshire RG1 8DE, UK
Tel: +44 118 950 8261